JOHN A. ROBINS

in collaboration with Trey Wilson

Find and Empower The Inner You

A compelling guide to success, happiness and stress-free living.

To Johanne,

Wishing you life-long happiness and fulfillment.

John A. Robins

Great IMPRESSIONS

First published by Great Impressions 2021

Copyright © 2021 by John A. Robins

All rights reserved. No part of this publication may be reproduced, stored or transmitted in any form or by any means, electronic, mechanical, photocopying, recording, scanning, or otherwise without written permission from the publisher. It is illegal to copy this book, post it to a website, or distribute it by any other means without permission.

John A. Robins asserts the moral right to be identified as the author of this work.

John A. Robins has no responsibility for the persistence or accuracy of URLs for external or third-party Internet Websites referred to in this publication and does not guarantee that any content on such Websites is, or will remain, accurate or appropriate.

Designations used by companies to distinguish their products are often claimed as trademarks. All brand names and product names used in this book and on its cover are trade names, service marks, trademarks and registered trademarks of their respective owners. The publishers and the book are not associated with any product or vendor mentioned in this book. None of the companies referenced within the book have endorsed the book.

First edition

This book is dedicated to my four children. James, Alexandra, Olivia, and Hannah. More than anything I hope you guys get to live successful, stress-free lives and enjoy lasting happiness. This book has been written to help you achieve these things.

Additionally, I hope the same for anyone that takes the time to read this book.

Contents

Preface — iv
Introduction — vii

1 Chapter 1 — 1
  The world, people, and things around you — 1
    What is life? — 1
    The goal of life — 2
    Observing and understanding experiences — 3
    What is the cause of stress and unhappiness? — 4
    Science, progress, and happiness — 4
    Comfort, pleasure, and happiness are very different things — 5
    Observe and understand the world around you — 6

2 Chapter 2 — 8
  It's All About You — 8
    Who are YOU? — 8
  Discovering The Inner-Self — 11
    What is the inner-self? — 11
    How to connect with the inner-self and experience self-awareness — 12
    Why is self-awareness so important? — 14
    Try to remain aware as often as possible — 15
    Benefits of constant self-awareness — 16
    Practice being self-aware and present whenever possible — 18
  Your Intellect — 19
    The three states of mind — 19
    Managing your intellect — 20
    Putting the past and the future into context — 21
  Your Emotions — 21

Understanding emotions	22
How do we know feelings of stress and anxiety are involuntary?	23
Dealing with simple negative emotions	23
Dealing with complex, lingering emotions	24
Techniques for dealing with negative emotions	26
How to meditate the right way	27
What about positive emotions	30
Your Ego	30
Identifying and understanding your ego	30
Attachments are the root cause of stress and anxiety	32
Your Body	34
Where does your body fit into all of this?	34
Now What?	35
Don't overthink	35
Before moving on	36
3 Chapter 3	37
The Importance of Education and Knowledge	37
Why jumping to conclusions can be a problem	37
The three perceptions of truth	38
Ignorance is definitely not bliss	40
Your reason for being	42
The joy of learning	43
A note on the word enlightenment	45
Intellect vs. intelligence vs. intellectual	46
The process of learning	47
Having the right mindset when it comes to knowledge	47
Too be (smart) or not to be - The choice is yours	48
Ten steps to learning the art of living and becoming 'enlightened.'	48
How much learning is required?	49
Support the education and growth of others	50
4 Chapter 4	52
The Art of Living	52
Prevention is better than cure	53

Coming to terms with the world YOU live In	54
Why do our intellects go on endless chatter loops?	56
The Importance of accepting what is	56
Time heals all wounds	59
When is good or bad, right or wrong, just different?	60
Analyzing and understanding your motives	61
Why does giving into desires only lead to short-term pleasures?	61
Giving really is better than receiving	62
Give consideration to your acts of kindness	63
Should you care what people think about you?	64
Why do so many evil people succeed?	65
Understanding and managing expectations	66
A simple way to improve your life immediately	67
Youth is wasted on the young (Wealth is wasted on the old!)	69
Life is all about your actions - A note on jobs and careers	71
Thinking beyond jobs and careers - What is YOUR purpose in life?	73
What makes more sense, spending less or more than you earn?	73
What else do you need to know?	75
5 Chapter 5	76
Reader's Questions Answered	76
Acknowledgments	91
About the Author	92

Preface

A note from John A. Robins

Like many people, I have spent countless years pondering the meaning of life and our reason for being. As a young man, I steered my career path toward maximizing income to buy things to make me happy and enjoy life in the lap of luxury. Despite having earned a respectable amount during my life (and spending nearly as much!) I still experienced sadness, anxiety, and stress. It became evident that making more money, buying more things, and satisfying my desires did not achieve lasting happiness and certainly did not reduce stress.

Eventually, I got to a point where I was just not happy with my life. Working so hard that I didn't have time to enjoy myself. Mortgage payments, school fees, drinking, and partying and yet, going nowhere. I decided it was time to simplify my life, let go of some of the baggage I was carrying and re-evaluate. Around the same time, I was introduced to several books that collectively changed my life. They gave me many of the answers I was looking for. Having read the books and gained a permanent mindset change, there were still a few things niggling me.

Firstly, none of the books provided a complete guide in themselves. Any one of them on their own would not have had the same effect. Secondly, the books were written with distracting references to god, spirituality or drawing power from the universe, etc. They were unnecessarily abstract - a whole bunch of borderline hocus-pocus unsubstantiated statements irrelevant to the core value of what I learned.

For many more years, I thought nothing of it. In general, following the principles I had learned, living a considerably better life as a result. And then COVID hit. Like many people, my life changed in an instant. My stress and anxiety levels hit the roof (as did my blood pressure). I had been knocked out of my comfort zone and drifted into a reactive state. For a short while, the impact of COVID made me lose touch with the techniques, guidelines, and principles I had learned earlier. I could see the potential of losing what I had built up over the last 15 years, and it really stressed me out. I was not in a good place.

During conversations with my colleagues at work, I realized I had allowed myself to be knocked off balance without even noticing. Since we were all living in uncertain times, I wanted to help my colleagues and I introduced the books that had the biggest impact on me. Taking time to review the books together, there was a consensus that while these books were good, their life-changing messages would be much better put together in a single publication, simplified and shortened, giving rise to a single comprehensive guide to living a successful, happy, stress-free life.

At the time of writing this, I am 61. I have had a full life with plenty of ups and downs, giving me the benefit of hindsight and years of experience at my disposal. When starting to write this book, the question that kept coming to mind was, how do I write a book for young people so that a) it will resonate and b) that they can see the value of learning and practicing the art of living the right way, in a way that the reader can determine for themselves rather than be told? I decided to ask one of my colleagues to join me in writing the book. Trey Wilson, a young man in his late twenties, just starting to ponder the meaning of life and reason for being, reminiscent of me in my early days. By collaborating on this book, I felt we would be able to incorporate the knowledge and wisdom I had gained over the years and present it so that today's young and future generations will want to read, enjoy, and hopefully benefit. This book is the result of that collaboration.

A note from Trey Wilson

Not knowing is the simplest mistake a person can make. It is only a matter of research and understanding that separates foolish belief from concrete evidence and efficient living. I believe for most people, the key to life is to get a good job, a family, and have friends and experiences to keep the show going. Yet, they have already made a simple mistake. What happens when those very things work against you and deprive you of happiness instead of providing it? That's a thought I've always had. I've always wanted to act on it and just didn't know-how.

My goal in life now is to alleviate all forms of stress, pain, sorrow, etc. Just one big goal. Everything else just falls under secondary goals, such as the purchase of a new home. The one thing that I've noticed is that the world we live in doesn't promote this way of thinking and living because we are in a monetary world. Falling victim to the ways of today's society, I'm in a constant battle to remain peaceful and unbothered by outside forces that have no regard for my mental quietude.

Meeting John helped me realize that I had temporarily placed that task on hold to indulge in more things to potentially break my peace. Given a couple of books to read, it has opened my mind to a new perspective and acted as a guide to a calmer me. This has been initiated in earlier efforts by physiologists and therapists but only resonated with practical speech and proper delivery of the concept. I don't have the experience in life that John has, but that's grounds for a new perspective and an invigorating conversation.

Introduction

Living is an art. Most people are unaware of this. We are born, grow up, and go about our day-to-day activities without any formal training on how to make the most of our lives. Our parents coach us based on their experiences, and schools attempt an academic education. For the rest, we assume we have to make it up and learn as we go. No wonder we don't do a good job. So many people feel stress, anxiety, and sadness. The solution is to learn and practice the art of living, in the same way we need to learn and practice any skill to become good at it. Why should we expect life to be any different?

This book is entirely for your benefit and is a guide to finding and empowering the inner you, leading to a lasting happy, stress-free life. It helps you identify the primary causes of anxiety, stress, and unhappiness in your life. It gives you an overview of the benefits of understanding and learning the art of living, and it provides you with a range of tools and techniques to learn and practice the art of living. **As with any learning, acquiring the theory and then putting it into practice provides a complete educational journey.** In this case, the destination is achieving success, experiencing lasting happiness, and living a stress-free life.

The book is presented so that you can investigate, analyze, and verify the knowledge provided. **Learning and understanding can only be achieved when starting from what you already know to be true, leading you to what is currently unknown to you so that it can become known, verified, and then practiced.** This knowledge will guide you in a similar way to guiding a tourist to a museum. If you tell the tourist that the museum is to the left of the bus station, if the tourist does not know where the bus station is, then the location remains unknown. However, if the tourist knows where the clock tower is and you say that the museum is behind the clock tower, they have now learned what was previously unknown in relation to what they already knew. This book will highlight what you already know or can observe for yourself and guide you to understanding what is currently unknown to you.

Verify everything and maximize your application of independent thought. The key to success is relying on your own judgment. As with developing any valuable skill, the process of learning, digesting, and practicing takes time, for some, a lot of time. Stick with it and remember to test, experiment, and verify your progressive increase in knowledge and understanding through practical application in your day-to-day living. **You will see for yourself that as you develop the art of living, the power within you will be released and will, in turn, be used to your advantage**.

The book is logically structured around five chapters. The objective of chapter one is to give you a guide to understanding the world around you and how you fit into the world. Chapter two aims to provide you with a deeper understanding of yourself and how you connect with the world around you. Chapter 3 explains the importance of education and verification and how it provides you additional support to help you achieve happiness. Chapter five is made up of questions that friends and family have asked after reading the first four chapters.

As you progress through the book you will be challenged, asked a number of questions, and set a series of exercises. All of which will guide you to finding and empowering the inner-you.

1

Chapter 1

The world, people, and things around you

The objective of this chapter is to give you the opportunity to examine, think about, and better understand the world around you, and most importantly, work out how it relates to you in your pursuit of happiness. To get the most out of this chapter, think about how each of the sections below relates to your own life as well as the life of others around you. Does it resonate with you, can you verify the statements made in this chapter, do you have your own examples that allow you to verify what is written here?

Observing and understanding the people and world around you gives you tools to help you understand how you fit into the world and examine your relationships with the people and objects that exist around you.

What is life?

To be good at life, you need to have some understanding of what it is. The dictionary definition of life is, *"the condition that distinguishes animals and plants from inorganic matter, including the capacity for growth, reproduction, functional activity, and continual change preceding death."*

In Sanskrit, one of the world's oldest languages, the definition is simpler,

"life is a stream of experiences."

As long as experiences flow, there is life. When the flow of experiences end, then there is death. An experience is, therefore, a unit of life.

A unit of life, or an experience, comprises two components, the subject, and the object. The individual, you, is the subject. The world and things around you, the object. When you, the subject, interacts with the object it gives rise to your experiences. **The flow of your experiences is your life.**

The goal of life

In the absence of being presented a 'user manual' when we are born providing us with a detailed brief and plan explaining why we are here, what we are meant to achieve in life, and for what purpose, it is by nature left up to us to decide what goals to set for ourselves. Interestingly, when you examine the goals people set for themselves, you see that they all lead to the same overriding singular objective, regardless of **whether people are looking for wealth, fame, to change the world, or to help others. Indeed, whatever goal people set for themselves, in the end, they are all aimed at achieving one thing, lasting happiness for themselves.** That being the case, it is logical to consider that since trying to find lasting happiness is what we do naturally, that in fact, the goal of life is for all of us to find lasting happiness.

Finding lasting happiness for yourself is not as selfish as it may at first seem. **When you become truly happy and live your life in peace and without stress, you find that you are better equipped to help those around you and give back to the world. You become a beacon for people to admire and follow.** In the same way that learning to live the right way will improve your productivity, it increases the positive contribution you make to the world. You may recall the safety instructions given on an aircraft. You are advised to place your oxygen mask over your own face first before helping others. It ensures that you are safe and in a better position to help others. The same is true in life.

Observing and understanding experiences

There are three types of experiences, physical, emotional, and intellectual. The quality and quantity of these experiences determine your perception of the world and your life. If your experiences at any given time seem happy, then you are happy. If your experiences at any given time generate anger, then you are angry. If your experiences are exciting, then your life is exciting. If your experiences are boring, then you are bored. It stands to reason then that most people believe by increasing the number of happy experiences in their lives, they will become increasingly happy and satisfied. So the endless loop of trying to fill our lives with happy experiences through wealth, comfort, and short-term pleasures begins.

The problem is, this fails to consider a) we do not analyze in advance the long-term effect of getting what we desire and b) that we do not control all that goes on around us or what happens in our lives. Therefore, **as we cannot control everything that happens around us to ensure we remain happy, given that an experience is an interaction between ourselves and the world around us (the subject and the object). Perhaps it makes more sense to realize that if we cannot control the world and happenings around us, maybe the source of lasting happiness is within us**.

What is the cause of stress and unhappiness?

A reliable starting point for learning the art of living is for you to study the world, objects, and people around you and your relationship with them. On close examination, **you will find that it is not the world, things, or people that bother you in the way you think, but your relationship with them due to your current level of knowledge and understanding.** Anxiety, stress, anger, and sorrow, all the things that make you unhappy, are caused by your resistance to accept what is or your desire to control what will be. To achieve lasting happiness, you will need to learn how to observe, accept and put into context your experiences and refine your relationship with the world, objects, and people around you. As you do this, you will see how stress reduces and happiness increases.

Science, progress, and happiness

Throughout history, people have studied the world (the subject) and endeavored to make changes and advancements to provide us greater happiness. Since the 1800s, scientists and industrialists have created a near-perfect world providing great convenience and comfort to our lives. Despite this progress, many people remain sad and stressed; there is still an abundance of worry, anxiety, suffering, and sorrow everywhere. Philosophers, on the other hand, have spent their time studying humans, the subject. Both ancient and modern philosophers seem to arrive at the same conclusion, **humans are, for the most part, unprepared and untrained for life, giving rise to frustration, anxiety, and sorrow.** With the proper knowledge and training, individuals can encounter any experience and avoid frustration, anxiety, or stress.

The primary differentiation between humans and other animals is our ability to choose. Humans have evolved the capacity to choose their actions, and they need to make choices at almost every moment of their life. Animals, on the other hand, are preprogrammed and do not have the dilemma of choosing their actions. A wolf cannot become a vegetarian, or a rabbit become a meat-eater. **Practicing the art of living trains you to choose the right course of action in every circumstance or experience**, in your home, at work, in society, everywhere.

Comfort, pleasure, and happiness are very different things

Money does not buy happiness, but it does make misery easier to cope with!
 Money, as we all know, can significantly increase our comfort levels. A lovely home, a delightful garden, perhaps a gardener, a cleaner; all these things make life easier and more comfortable. However, this is not happiness. We can have all of these things and still feel bored, sad, or unhappy. Money also buys bursts of pleasure. For example, buying new clothes, a new car, or purchasing a holiday. While buying these things gives us shots of joy, they do not give rise to lasting happiness. Clothes get worn and need to be replaced. Cars get old and break down. Holidays last for short periods before your everyday life kicks back into play. For many, just keeping up the payments on money borrowed to buy the things they believe will make them happy can lead to stress, anxiety, and sadness. Ironic!

Even if you have the money for these things and can afford to keep replacing them, when we observe people with wealth, power, or fame, many of their stories indicate a high degree of anxiety, distress, and sadness. **Through simple observation and study, it is clear that wealth, houses, cars or other purchases, or even relationships do not lead to lasting happiness. We all discover that it is much more complex than that**. Many other factors are at play when looking for lasting happiness. Unfortunately, many do not realize there is no lasting satisfaction through acquisition or short-term pleasures. The quest for happiness through wealth, fame, and possessions becomes an ever-spinning treadmill.

As clearly demonstrated, **increased comfort and shots of pleasure are not the same as, nor do they lead to, lasting happiness or a stress-free life**. By observing our own life and the lives of others, we can see this is true because we all experience it one way or another. One classic example of this is the child that is desperate to have a pet explaining how happy they will become, only to find that months or years later the pet becomes taken for granted and even a source of burden as it requires feeding and looking after every day. Or the adult who believes true happiness is dependent on marrying a particular person only to find years later the stress of thinking their happiness is dependent on divorcing that same person.

Through our experiences as we grow up, and because we know no better, we are lulled into thinking that the more money we earn, the more comfort we buy, and the more pleasures we experience, the happier we will become. Yet, what we actually experience is short-term pleasures and the ongoing flow of the resulting stresses and anxiety we put ourselves through trying to earn more money to increase our levels of comfort or increase the number of short-term pleasures. Society as a whole is under the naive belief that if we keep going we can earn enough money to achieve lasting happiness. This quest becomes never-ending. There is nothing inherently wrong with increasing one's level of comfort or enjoying short-term pleasures. However, **if you recognize through your own experiences that the more you get, the more you want. If you are aware that true happiness lies within you rather than through external comforts or pleasures, you can begin the journey of finding lasting happiness.**

Observe and understand the world around you

Taking the time out to actively watch and study the world around you will help you gain a better understanding of how the world works. People watching is something we all do. Some do it consciously and consider it a hobby. Others do it more casually and subconsciously. The reason we do it naturally is to gain a better understanding of people and the world around us, which in turn can teach us to interact with the world better and achieve better outcomes.

One technique for examining the world around you and watching people is to start by observing the people closest to you, both at work and at home.

CHAPTER 1

See what pushes their buttons, and in particular, try and identify the exact moment and cause of any sparks that in turn cause animated reactions. **Getting to the root cause of a reaction to an experience is important, and watching it happen in others can help you be more conscious of seeing it in yourself.** No doubt we have all witnessed people going ballistic at some poor unsuspecting customer service rep on the other end of a phone. The chances of that rep being able to change company policy or operate outside of the instructions they have been given is slim to none. In any situation though, shouting at them and getting angry with them is highly unlikely to get a positive response and is definitely going to reduce that person's interest in trying to help.

Observe the world around you, observe the people around you, observe your own behavior and experiences. On close examination, you will see that lasting happiness can never be achieved by increasing your comfort levels or experiencing an endless stream of short-term pleasures. Take this opportunity to stop, rethink, and consider that through understanding and learning how to re-evaluate your relationships with the world, people, and things around you, you may find a better path to living a lasting successful, happy, stress-free life.

2

Chapter 2

It's All About You

If people, things, and the world around you are not the solution to achieving success and lasting happiness, the answer must lie within you. The objective of this chapter is to give you the opportunity to gain a deeper understanding of yourself and provide techniques to help you live a happier life. As you read the sections below, take the time to consider if the statements made make sense and directly relate to you. Your happiness depends upon it.

Who are YOU?

The short answer to this question is that you are the sum of all the components that make up who you are. Sorry for the abstract answer, but the point is, this answer identifies that **to really understand who you are, you need to be aware of, and connect with, all your component parts. You also need to be aware of how they interact with each other and the world around you.**

People are incredibly complex bioelectrochemical organisms. To go into detail about what makes up a person. To explain how emotions are created and how the brain interprets them. And, to explain how the external world is experienced through our five biological senses and transferred into bio-electrochemical signals and impulses which turn into emotional and physical reactions would lead to a book that would make the novel War and Peace seem like a quick read by comparison. Fortunately, it's not necessary to go into this much detail, any more than you need to understand a complete list of components or the workings of a car or a laptop to be able to use them effectively. **We can identify the summary elements that make us up using simple references that we all know and understand to be true.**

We are all generally aware that we are made up of two main components. One, the Body, that is, the physical component of who we are, and two, the mind, the non-physical part of us, which makes sense of and interprets what is going on around us and what we are feeling. Beyond these two core components, who we are can be further subdivided as follows:

- <u>Body</u>	- Physical Presence
	- Emotions
YOU - <u>Mind</u>	- Memory
	- Ego
	- Conscience
	- Intellect
- <u>Inner-self</u>	- Pure Consciousness

<u>Your Physical Presence</u> refers to your body parts, including your sense organs that enable the five senses. It is your apparatus for interacting and communicating with the world through sounds and actions and the home of your mind, the brain.

Your Emotions are your primal physiological responses to your experiences as detected by your senses.

Your Memory is, of course where you store your recollection of the past and where you store what you learn. While human memory does a pretty good job of storing our experiences, the most important thing to know about your memory is that it is not completely reliable.

Your Ego is where you store the image of yourself, others, objects, and the world around you. Your personal reference library, which in part is present when you are born (your primal instinct, nature), and in part, is what you build from your experiences throughout your lifetime (nurture). It includes all your dogma and preconceptions, whether they are right or wrong.

Your Conscience is also part nature, part nurture. It's how you determine right or wrong. It's your moral value reference point. When you know deep down you are doing something wrong, or you see someone else doing something wrong and something is nagging at you telling you that it might not be such a good idea or that maybe you should step in and prevent it, that's your conscience. Interestingly, it becomes much louder when you are present and aware.

Your Intellect is the part of you that interprets and rationalizes information and experiences, compares them with your ego's picture of the world, and directs the body to judge, act, or react.

Your Inner-self is pure consciousness. The real you and the part of you that connects you with everything around you.

Yes, this breakdown is a somewhat simplistic labeling of the parts that make you up, and there are some overlaps between these components. However, recognizing these core components in this way allows you to progress from the known (the body and mind) to the unknown (our inner-self and becoming self-aware). **Only when you recognize and are fully connected to all your parts can you start to feel and listen to what they are each telling you and start the process of learning the right way to live in turn releasing the power that lies within you.**

Discovering The Inner-Self

What is the inner-self?

When people are out of touch with their inner-self, they inherently feel that something is missing in their lives. This feeling creates the desire to fill the emptiness. Similar to the desire to eat when the stomach is empty, it is a natural instinct. These desires use the body to obtain sensual pleasure and the mind to experience emotional joy and intellectual, rational satisfaction. These desires are what trigger an insatiable quest, believing that additional comfort and a constant stream of short-term pleasures are what lead to happiness. As most of us find out sooner or later, this is not the case.

Throughout history, philosophers, psychologists, and others have tried to describe the inner-self. Some refer to it as the soul, others the spirit, others the essence of our being. The challenge is that **trying to describe the feeling of awakening and being connected to your inner-self to someone who is not aware of it or has not connected with it is like explaining the flavor of a fruit or other food item to someone who has never tasted it.** What makes it even more difficult is if the person trying to explain doesn't actually know themselves, which s is where confusion steps in. To experience the challenge of trying to explain a feeling or sense to someone a) when neither party knows, and b) when one party does not know, have a go at exercise 1, it's fun!

Exercise 1: Try for yourself. Find a food item that neither you nor a friend has tasted before. To start, without tasting the item, both of you try describing its flavor. Of course, that is impossible. Now, one of you taste the item and try to describe its flavor to the other. You will instinctively try to explain the flavor by referring to other foods that you and your friend have tasted before (the known). It may be sweet, sour, savory, salty, earthy, or buttery. But after all the references given in words, your friend will still not know the exact flavor until they try it for themselves. The same is true with identifying and connecting with the inner-self. It is not a string of words that you can understand. The inner-self is something you have to experience yourself to come to know it, and **you will know it when you experience it.**

The first thing to be aware of is that your inner-self is not the voice inside your head you use for reviewing and rationalizing experiences as most believe. That is your intellect, just one part of your mind, and YOU can learn to control it in the same way you learn to control your body.

For most people, an uncontrolled mind leads to anxiety and unhappiness. Perhaps constantly going over and over bad experiences from the past, leading to what we call regret. Or, envisaging bad experiences you think may occur in the future, referred to as worry. Mark Twain brilliantly expressed this phenomenon in his famous quote,

> "I've lived through some terrible things in my life, some of which actually happened."

How to connect with the inner-self and experience self-awareness

For some, experiencing self-awareness and separating the inner-self from their mind for the first time can be achieved quickly with a simple exercise. For others, it can take longer and require several exercises. Some people never manage it. **However, be aware that becoming self-aware is essential before moving forward and releasing the power within you.**

Excise 2 below is a simple method for discovering and connecting with the inner-you. Try this simple exercise below now and see if it works for you the first time around.

CHAPTER 2

Exercise 2: This exercise is designed to lead you from the known to what is unknown to you and help you become aware of the inner-self:

1. Read the following steps slowly and deliberately.
2. As you read these words, find and listen to the voice in your mind, reading out the words.
3. Observe. Listen to each word as your mind is reading them.
4. Now ask yourself this question. If your mind is reading out these words, who is it listening to them?
5. The answer, your inner-self. Be conscious of the fact that your MIND is reading the words and that your inner-self is consciously listening to them.
6. At the same time, as the inner-self is listening to your mind reading these words, become aware of yourself in your surroundings.
7. Close your eyes for a moment, sense yourself and the environment around you. When you open your eyes again,
8. Become aware and observe yourself. Sense your presence in the space you are in and remain aware of YOUR mind reading to YOU.
9. Become conscious of what else is going on around you. Keep listening to yourself reading while you are doing this.
10. As you carry out this exercise, you become the observer. As the observer, you can sense all of these things, including your voice and yourself in the space around you. You are connecting with the observer, the inner-self. And you are allowing the inner-self to become awake, conscious.
11. Stop reading for a moment, count to 10 slowly. Listen to the numbers as you count. You are now directly conscious of the fact that you are not the voice in your mind. You are now controlling the voice. The inner-you is now controlling your mind and being self-aware.
12. Now stop the voice. Make your voice silent. See how long you can keep your voice silent before it spontaneously starts up again. This step shows you how your mind is constantly trying to chatter. But remember, you can stop it for as long as you want. It just takes practice.
13. Go one step further. If there is someone in the room you can talk to, strike

up a conversation. Observe both sides of the conversation, observe what that person is saying, observe what you are thinking and saying back to them. If there is no one in the room, call up a friend, observe yourself on the phone, and envisage your friend on the other end of the phone.

If you were able to identify and sense the inner-you listening to the words as your intellect read them out in your mind and if the inner-you was at the same time able to observe your mind, body, and the surroundings around you; remaining conscious of what was going on around you. And if the inner-you that watched both sides of a conversation between your intellect and another person, **then you have awoken the inner-self and experienced self-awareness.**

Try listening to the voice in your mind as often as you can, and try to pause it for as long as you can and experience the world around you. Be aware of others. Observe them and yourself as you interact. **The more you practice, the more frequently you will become self-aware.** This step is just the beginning.

Experiencing self-awareness is essential to being able to learn the art of living. If this exercise has not worked for you, do it again more slowly, spending more time identifying the voice in your mind reading the words. Keep trying. Once you have connected with the voice in your mind, progress to step 3 in the exercise and keep going.

Why is self-awareness so important?

Waking the inner-self and experiencing self-awareness are important for three main reasons. First, it provides first-hand experience and knowledge that there is an inner-self. It verifies your understanding of the core parts that make you up, i.e., 1) Body (arms, legs, sensory organs, etc.). 2) Mind (emotions, intellect, and ego), and 3) your inner-self (the observer, the controller, your core being).

Second, it demonstrates **you are not your mind. Your mind is a separate**

part of you, like your body, that YOU can control rather than the other way around.

Thirdly, it puts you in a better position to observe and question what is going on around you, your actions, and your reactions. You may be aware of the anecdote about a young woman that always cut the front and back end off of a turkey before putting it into the oven. One thanksgiving the woman's mother was preparing lunch with her and asked why she did this. The daughter replied that she had always done it and remembered watching her mother do it when she was growing up. The mother laughed and explained to the daughter that she only did it because, in those days, their oven was very small, and the turkey would not fit in. The woman never thought to question this. She merely blindly copied what she saw without ever giving it a single thought. That is how so many people live their lives.

You cannot fully understand or practice the right way to live unless you become self-aware, any more than you can study at school while you are asleep. **You need to unlock and release your mind first so that the real you can take control of your mind and develop your component parts rather than letting your mind control you and them.**

Try to remain aware as often as possible

Remaining constantly aware and controlling your mind is challenging. Initially, you will find it hard to stay self-aware for anything more than short periods, minutes even, as your mind will naturally start to wander. Even after experiencing self-awareness, you will find that constantly becoming aware and controlling your mind rather than letting your mind control you takes time and practice.

Have you ever been making your way to a familiar location? Perhaps walking, cycling, or driving, it doesn't matter which, and then when you arrived not remembered the journey? Or have you ever been lost in your mobile phone, perhaps playing a game or chatting with a friend, and lost all sense of time and place? Or have you gone to a room to do or look for something and then got there and wondered what it was? These are all examples of how your mind constantly distracts you. In many instances, actively working against you, leading you into a mind loop, constantly evaluating a happening from the past, or concerning you with an event you are expecting in the future. **Understanding your mind and how it distracts and controls you is information that can help the inner-you take back control.**

Benefits of constant self-awareness

There are numerous benefits to being self-aware and living in the present, and actively conscious of what is going on around you. For a start, it means that you spend more time living in the real world around you rather than in your mind. It gives you the thrill of living and enjoying your life as it happens rather than sleepwalking through it. Life becomes so much more enjoyable. It becomes brighter and more vibrant. Furthermore, it allows the inner-self to observe, connect with and understand what is going on around you to a higher level, and it gives you the power to better manage your reactions to what is happening around you.

You have probably come across the expression - think before you speak. Well, next time you are having a conversation with someone, actively awaken the inner-self. Observe the conversation you are having as it is taking place. Observe what the other person is saying and observe yourself, your body language, and the words you are saying. Become aware of the different responses you can give. Rather than automatically responding with the first words that come into your mind, pause a moment and choose the most appropriate for the conversation's outcome. You will find that being self-aware, the observer, you have much more control over the outcome of the discussion. You can choose to make the person feel more loved or more appreciated. If the person is agitated, you will find that you will have the power to make them either more agitated (rarely a benefit) or more relaxed. **As you practice becoming aware and conscious more frequently, and by awakening the inner-you, everything around you becomes more enjoyable.**

You will become more observant and aware of things going on around you. Most importantly, you will begin to free the power in you, giving rise to a more beneficial impact on what is going on around you, your life will start to become less stressful, and you will experience more joy.

In addition to naturally reducing your desires as you recognize you do not need possessions to be happy, remaining self-aware also makes you more productive. Ironically, enabling you to earn more and increase your wealth. **As you master the art of living, your productivity increases due to three skills you will progressively strengthen**. The three Cs. They are your concentration, consistency, and cooperation.

Concentration is the act of keeping your mind centered on a particular task at hand. Even while reading this book, you may find yourself drifting off into thoughts about past events. Perhaps how you might have handled something differently or how someone mistreated you. Maybe your mind is drifting off into the future, thinking about what to have for dinner, worrying about a client or an upcoming meeting. It is natural for the mind to constantly wander into the past or the future. However, this is something you can learn to manage. **Developing techniques to control your mind and keep it focused improves your performance significantly.** It is one of the numerous techniques to help you reduce stress and take more control over your life.

Consistency is the action of maintaining your efforts on a particular set goal. **In the same way, water falling in the same place on a rock wears a channel for it to flow, or when the sun, concentrated through a magnifying glass, can cause things to burn. When your energies become focused, they also become more powerful**. In today's complex world, we are constantly bombarded with distractions. At a time in history when we were promised ease and simplicity with the introduction of digital technology, in fact, our lives seem to have become more complex than ever. We are all constantly bombarded by things that need to be done before we get a moment to allocate time to focus on things that are truly important to us. Learning how to manage time, becoming more consistent and focused on the things that truly matter, identifying and eliminating time-wasting activities in your life significantly contribute to you becoming more productive.

Cooperation is the act of achieving goals and completing tasks while working with other people. TEAM - Together, Everyone Achieves More. Teams and organizations achieve more than working as individuals. In many instances, there is a natural tendency to get things done on our own. We feel that the time it takes to train someone to help us or pay someone in addition to ourselves is less beneficial than working on our own. Increasing your spirit of cooperation and refining the skill of bringing people together with complementary capabilities to get work done faster and to a higher standard is another significant move towards increased productivity.

Practice being self-aware and present whenever possible

Exercise 2 above is just one technique for actively awakening the inner-you. If that worked for you, you will find that with practice you can bring yourself back into self-awareness within moments at any time. **Other techniques allow you to become both self-aware and more present, which will help you release your inner-self even further from your mind.** Exercise 3 below is designed to help you silence your mind and ensure that you are in the present.

Exercise 3: Start by watching yourself as you do things. Perhaps at first, watch your hands typing the words on a keyboard or washing your hands in a sink. Don't just look at your hands. Sense and observe the inner-you controlling and washing your hands, what you are doing with them and how you are doing it. Sense the touch of the keyboard on the ends of your fingers or the water flowing over your hands. As you are doing this, simultaneously listen to and be aware of all the other things happening around you. The point is, this practice will help you go beyond being self-aware to becoming fully aware, fully conscious, and fully present. Observe all the little details in the process.

When you start becoming self-aware, it is easy to go beyond this and, at the same time, become fully aware of both you and what is going on around you, making you fully present and establishing complete consciousness. The more you practice, the more natural it becomes.

Your Intellect

The three states of mind

People live in one of three states of mind. Knowing these three states and identifying what state your mind is in will help you think about how to ensure you remain in the best possible state of mind at all times.

One state of mind is the untrained, unsettled mind, constantly churning and chattering and agonizing over past events or worrying about events that may or may not occur in the future; spending little or no time in the present. This person's mind is constantly on the go. In this state of mind, the individual continually feels anxiety, anger, unease, worry, or regret, etc. The mind in this state is literally out of control, and the constant chatter of the intellect allows no peace. This state of mind is like a cone standing on its point. Completely unstable and constantly churning.

The second state of mind is what most people live in. It is like a cone lying on its side. The mind is generally more at rest in this state, carrying out day-to-day activities in a stable fashion. Perhaps chattering to itself in the background. However, if external events upset or rock the mind in this state, it becomes unstable, rolling and rocking backward and forwards as it is buffeted by external events knocking into it.

Finally, the fully-trained and aware mind is like a cone sitting on its base. Completely stable. Regardless of what is going on around, it remains firm and in place. This state is achieved by having a trained mind. It enables you to view and handle anything that goes on around you and remains entirely stable and unfazed. Untrained and unmanaged, your emotions, intellect, and ego work against you resulting in anxiety, stress, and unhappiness. Training your mind to become stable is a key step in achieving lasting happiness and living a stress-free life.

Managing your intellect

We are taught that time is made up of three dimensions. An enormous past that has gone on for millions of years, a future that, as far as we know, will never end, and then the present, a fleeting moment that resides between the two. **The fact is, when you think about it, the past does not exist any more than a sandwich does after you have eaten it. Once consumed, it's gone. Nor does the future exist, any more than your sandwich did before it was made!** The only point in time that exists is now, and as odd as it may seem, you have only ever existed in the present moment, and you always will. However, left to its own devices, your intellect tends to enjoy being distracted and jumps through time at will. It may spend time replaying happenings of the past or playing out possible occurrences in the future.

It is easy to let your mind get lost with any number of distractions, and the fact is, there is no harm in allowing your mind to review the past or the present from time to time when your inner-self is aware of it and managing it. However, if your mind is constantly being distracted, if you are not consistently self-aware, and if your inner-self is not in control, then your mind, by definition, is out of control. Meaning, **you are not consciously living your 'real' life at all, you are merely sleepwalking through your real-life living in your mind at random points in time**. Therefore, managing your intellect means ensuring that the inner-you, the observer, is in control of you, that you are consistently self-aware, and that you are living in the present rather than letting your mind drift off into the past or the future.

Putting the past and the future into context

Learning from the past and being prepared for the future are essential activities. The thing is, you can do these things while being aware and in the present. It is not necessary to allow your mind to drift off into and dwell on the past or the future. Allowing your mind to wander aimlessly in a loop, playing over the same old scenarios, again and again, perhaps obsessing over past mistakes or worrying about possible future events.

Learning from the past is what teaches us not to make the same mistakes in the future. However, what has happened in the past has happened. Constantly playing out the same scenarios of the past time after time will not change what happened. It is pointless and leads directly to stress and anxiety. Working out how to correct errors you have made in the past is, of course, helpful, and planning for the future means that you can be better prepared for what might lie ahead. Whether it is choosing what to eat for dinner while preparing your shopping list or making sure you have prepared for an upcoming meeting or trip. But constantly obsessing or worrying over what the future may or may not hold is pointless. It, too, leads to anxiety or stress.

The key to gaining control, learning, and practicing the art of living is to actively live in the present and remain aware at all times, allowing yourself planned periods to reflect on the past so that you can learn from it and prepare for the future to reduce negative outcomes. That is as far as you should go. Whenever possible, keep yourself in the present and control your mind.

Our minds constantly chatter most of the time, and we tend to only partially notice the world around us. Sure, we see it there, we know what is around us, but we do not fully connect with our surroundings until we actively awaken the inner-self and actively look at our surroundings while being present and aware.

Your Emotions

Understanding emotions

We all experience emotions at some point or another in our lives. And there are many different types of emotions that we get to experience — anger, hate, love, excitement, fear, etc. Some feelings we get to enjoy like love and pleasure, others we would be better off without; anger and hatred for example. Fortunately, in the same way that you can awaken your inner-self and become self-aware by observing your inner voice chattering. You can also separate your inner-self from your emotions, allowing you to monitor and manage them. Before being able to handle your emotions effectively, it helps to understand them and why you feel them.

The relationship between your intellect, ego, body, and emotions is complex. **Emotions are involuntary and arise from physiological changes in your body when witnessing or experiencing a particular event around you that provokes or challenges your ego, intellect, or combination of both.** It might be an encounter with an attractive member of the opposite sex, or it could be the person next to you stealing your lunch. This triggering or challenging disrupts the brain's limbic system, which comprises the hippocampus, amygdala, hypothalamus, and thalamus, the areas responsible for emotional processing and our fight or flight response, the ancient physiological response to threat. Once disrupted, the brain's limbic system triggers a reaction in our autonomic nervous system. It increases the level of adrenaline in the bloodstream, raising heart rate and blood pressure, causing shallow, rapid breathing. It also reduces blood levels around your stomach and other digestive organs, pushing blood away from the digestive system. Because in essence, digestion is needed far less for survival than being able to run away or fight.

A severe reaction to an external event can lead to panic attacks and even hyperventilation. With most day-to-day events, the physical sensation is more mild, like butterflies, a knot in the stomach, or a lump in the throat. The intellect then interprets these feelings as fear, excitement, or anxiety, depending on the event that triggered the response. **Interestingly, fear and excitement are physiologically the same feelings. It is the intellect that interprets in your mind if the feeling is fear or excitement.** That is why some people experience fear when they are about to bungee jump and back out, and others feel excitement and go for the jump. As the saying goes, it's all in the mind.

Even though feelings of stress and anxiety are involuntary physiological responses to external events, there are several ways these feelings can be managed or even made disappear altogether.

How do we know feelings of stress and anxiety are involuntary?

Have you ever watched a TV program or a fictional movie where the storyline has made you cry because it was sad and emotional, or perhaps you felt angry because an injustice was being portrayed? The thing is, your intellect knows that the movie is entirely fictional, and yet, you still have these feelings. That is because these feelings are involuntary. Even though you may witness experiences that are entirely fictional, your involuntary emotional responses are real. However, what is particularly interesting is that because your intellect is aware that what you see in movies or in TV series is fictional, it does not make you act or react to what is going on.

Dealing with simple negative emotions

For the most part, simple emotions like anger and excitement flare up quickly. The good news is, they also tend to be short-lived, centered around the incident that triggered them. With time and practice, these simple emotions can be prevented before they start by re-programming your intellect and ego not to react to trivial, unimportant events. If you have not reached that stage, even when those emotions flare up, they can be quickly dissipated when you become self-aware and present before you react. To a self-aware and present person, these types of emotions are no longer important. They are no longer phased, disrupted, or upset by such feelings. The next time you feel a hint of anger or anxiety, immediately make yourself self-aware and present and assess your situation. Determine for yourself using your intellect what would be the best reaction to have to ensure the best outcome for you and the people around you. **A fully self-aware and fully present individual can manage the relationship between themselves and the objects, people, and things around them in real-time.** Nothing phases them, nothing destabilizes them, and they remain calm at all times no matter what is happening around them. Like a cone sitting on its base. Achieving this level of mental stability can take years of practice. Many of us may never fully get to this level, but that does not mean we should stop trying. Even before you develop the ability to remain constantly self-aware and fully present, you can significantly improve how you deal with your emotions after they have affected you.

Dealing with complex, lingering emotions

Complex emotions like regret, stress, and deep-rooted anxiety can creep up on you and linger. Most often, they are negative feelings caused by unhelpful attachments to things such as your ego, beliefs, possessions, people, pets, etc. These emotions can run deep and be far more challenging to manage. The most painful feelings we experience also trigger the intellect to chatter around negative thoughts, amplifying the emotions. It creates a feedback loop that without management we find hard to escape. Our mind in this scenario is working against us. A negative emotion triggers the intellect to race into negative thoughts. In turn, the negative thoughts intensify the negative feelings in our bodies. That is why **feelings of depression and anxiety tend to get worse rather than better over time until enough time passes where we naturally let go of these feelings.** If you have not reached the stage where you can intercept emotions before they affect you, break the emotional-intellect feedback loop, and take back control from your chattering mind.

Making sure we become self-aware and in the present is the only way to start dealing with emotions. The first step is to become self-aware and pause the chattering intellect. Second, separate your inner-self from the feelings of your emotions. Identify and observe the sensations inside you rather than react to them. Once you become the observer and pause your intellect and sense what you are feeling, you can take the time to observe what your unaware reaction would be to these feelings had it not been for the inner-you being awake and taking control. It's a bit like being a parent and stepping in between two bickering children. You get them to stop what they are doing and be quiet. You stand them apart and advise them to calm down and reflect. In effect, you are doing the same with your intellect and emotions. The inner you is stepping in to observe and control them. **Unmanaged, your emotions get more intense and start controlling you. When you monitor and manage your intellect and sense and reflect on what you are feeling, you can start to keep your emotions in check and begin the process of analyzing, re-evaluating, and resetting.**

In many situations, stepping in and taking control will enable you to calm down, connect with the inner-you, bring yourself into the present, and dissipate negative emotional feelings. Have you ever watched a TV program where a person is sitting calmly in a room and when they receive some terrible news, or something upsets them, they immediately start smashing things around them or punch a hole in the wall, or they start throwing things around the room? All these reactions are counterintuitive, counterproductive and generally lead to even more grief, anxiety, or other issues that they will have to deal with down the line. Firstly, it's pretty evident that breaking things when angry or upset never improves a situation or how you feel about it. Nor does it change the event that took place in the past or improve the outcome moving forward. Ultimately, it does not contribute positively to any outcome in any way. Watching other people get angry or smashing things around will increasingly bemuse you as you become more self-aware and fully present. You will quickly identify other people, both fictional and real, that are clearly out of control, letting their minds control them, often making things worse for themselves rather than better. You may even come to realize that once, in the past, that would be you.

Suppose your emotions run deep, causing anxiety or regret, and the feelings cannot be dissipated when observing. In this case, you will need to employ additional techniques to deal with your emotions. **There are several ways**

to manage negative emotions to prevent them from causing you stress or anxiety.

Techniques for dealing with negative emotions

Below is a list of ways you can manage negative emotional feelings. Just so that you know in advance, the first two solutions are not recommended!

One way is through the use of drugs. **Drugs such as cannabis and various opioids can disengage the automatic limbic and autonomic responses and replace feelings of anxiety and stress with chemicals that give feelings of joy and euphoria.** That is why many drug addicts use them to escape the pain, stress, and anxiety they are experiencing in their lives or to experience a constant artificial high. It's also why doctors prescribe them to patients with depression. They temporarily break the self-destructive loop between the event, the creation of feelings of stress and anxiety, and the chattering mind perpetuating and amplifying the body's reaction to the event.

Distracting your mind away from what is causing your anxiety and stress can also be a way of breaking the loop in some circumstances. Examples of this include watching a TV program or movie, going out with friends, engaging with social media, playing computer games, or even daydreaming. This is another reason why the untrained mind can become addicted to such activities. They can relieve stress. However, in turn, if it gets out of hand, they can lead to other issues of addiction to TV, mobile phones, or gaming machines, etc.

Exercise too is a good way of reducing feelings of stress and anxiety. Because feelings of anxiety or stress are triggered by our ancient fight or flight response, when we exercise, the body's autonomous nervous system assumes that we are 'running or fighting' to deal with the triggering event. Our mind also gets distracted away from the event, and as a result, the combination disarms the flight or fight response giving rise to feelings of joy and euphoria. Even if you are not feeling stress, exercise releases endorphins, making us feel good as a reward for looking after our body or responding to the fight or flight response. It is why for many people, exercise can also become a mild form of addiction.

Another way of dealing with feelings of stress and anxiety is through meditation. However, meditation is not what many people think it is. Many people are under the impression that meditation is a relaxation technique designed to put your mind into some form of trance-like state. Nothing could be further from the truth. Meditation is, in fact, a method for practicing deep self-awareness, being intensely present, and extending your consciousness to connect with everything around you as one technique for helping you fully connect with the inner-self and disconnect from your ego, emotions, and intellect. The relaxation comes from stopping your mind from chattering and allowing you to hold on to a much more extended period of awareness and presentness, and providing the opportunity to deal with your unwanted lingering negative emotions. There are different levels and types of meditation. The exercise below is a relatively basic form. As you increase your understanding of the best way to live life, meditation can contribute even further to achieving a state of lasting happiness.

How to meditate the right way

Try Exercise 4 below to see if you can get a sense of how meditation can help you manage your emotions.

Exercise 4: Lie down on your bed or sit in a comfortable chair and move your body around until you get yourself into a comfortable position. While a person experienced in meditation can pretty much meditate anywhere, at the outset, it is easier to start in a quiet, calming space so that you can focus on learning and developing your technique.

1. Just rest for a moment. Let your body settle into a comfortable position, and then close your eyes.
2. Listen to the voice in your mind and see if you can stop it from chattering. Early attempts at this are usually difficult, but it gets easier with practice.

Your mind wants to control you and will take any opportunity to chatter and distract you. If this happens, just keep interrupting the voice and make it stop.

3. Slow your breathing. Take in deeper, slower, but comfortable breaths. Hold your breath for just a moment as you switch from breathing in, to breathing out, and from breathing out, to breathing in. Another technique you can use for slowing your breath down and helping you stop your mind wandering is to count to three as you breathe in with your mind's voice and again as you breathe out. With you controlling your mind's voice by making it count, it cannot start to wander. You are now controlling it, not the other way around. It is one of the reasons some people chant the sound ohm constantly in their mind or while breathing out. It is chanted with the mind's voice to stop the Mind chattering, and it is chanted out loud as the resonance of the sound in the body has a calming and comforting effect and helps reduce the knot in your stomach. However, these are not essential elements of Meditation. Each person, over time, can develop their own techniques that work for them.

4. Once you are comfortable, have settled your mind, and started comfortable slow deep breaths, you can travel deeper into the meditation. With your eyes still closed, sense the presence of your body. There is no need to move any parts of your body. Just sense their existence. Start with your feet. Progressively move up your body, sensing your legs and knees, travel up further and sense your thighs then hands and arms. Then move up and sense your stomach and chest. Sense and feel your heart beating. Finally, your head. Having sensed each area of your body, sense and connect with all the areas of your body at the same time while continuing to take your deep but comfortable breaths.

5. Next, use your ears and senses to connect with the environment around you, making yourself profoundly present with no thoughts of the past or concerns of the future. Listen to and sense the environment you are in. Hear and sense the silence or faint noises that might be going on around you. Perhaps water flowing through radiators, air passing through an air-conditioning duct, etc. Next, listen, sense, and connect with what

is going on beyond the space you are in, wind noises, distant car noises, etc. Spend time to connect your mind with all that is going on around you and become intensely aware of your present moment.

6. The next step is to sense the emotions and feelings you are experiencing in your body. Perhaps the knot in your stomach, perhaps the lump in your throat, perhaps an elevated heartbeat. The primary significance of this part of the mediation technique is to identify that these feelings are not part of the inner-self. They are not YOU. They are merely separate feelings created by a physiological change in your body. By identifying and separating you from these feelings, you can start to dissipate them. Experiment with different breathing techniques, such as breathing in slowly through your nose, holding for a moment, and then exhaling quickly through your mouth. Experiment with chanting the letter ohm and allow the vibration of the sound to resonate through your chest and stomach. As you spend more time practicing, you will progressively find breathing techniques that work well for you in reducing the feelings of stress and anxiety in the body.

7. Once you have allocated as much time as you can focusing on the emotional feelings inside you and hopefully have reduced these feelings with regular slow breathing activity compared to when you started, you can open your eyes. Continue to remain self-aware and entirely present and slowly go about your day in the usual way.

Practice this form of meditation as often as you feel the need to calm your body. The more proficient you become, the easier it will be to identify your emotions as nothing more than physiological reactions in your body that you can reduce with regular meditation and breathing techniques.

What about positive emotions

Of course, emotions are not just negative. While negative emotions can lead to anxiety, stress, and even illness, positive emotions have the opposite effect. Laughter is the best medicine, as the saying goes. As noted above, watching TV or a movie can help distract you from feeling negative emotions. More than that, an uplifting, positive movie can actually make you feel better. The same as spending time with good friends that make you feel good. Allocating time to activities that generate positive emotions is a good thing until such time as you can develop the skillsets that put you into a position where you no longer have to experience negative emotions.

Your Ego

Identifying and understanding your ego

As noted earlier, your ego is part nature and part nurture. Your primal instincts are stored in your ego together with the life experiences that progressively build the image of who you think you are, the image you have created about the world around you, and the place where you store your beliefs and dogma. What is fascinating here is that **few people even begin to consider that their view of themselves, their view of the world around them, or their personal beliefs might be wrong**. Some do have what we refer to as a more open mind, and some may suspect in some corner of their mind that they do not have all the facts to be able to make a conclusive judgment on things. However, the natural instinct of the untrained and unmanaged mind is to assume that all they hold to be true is, in fact, true. When the ego is challenged, the untrained mind will instinctively and vehemently defend its vision, values, and beliefs, regardless of the truth. This too can lead to unnecessary anger, stress, and anxiety.

    History is littered with examples. When Galileo started publishing his findings of the earth orbiting the sun rather than the sun orbiting the earth, building on observations made by Copernicus and others before him, Galileo was sentenced to life imprisonment for questioning the beliefs held by the officials of the Catholic church at that time. Of course, we know today that Galileo was correct, not the Church. Michael Servetus, the scientist who discovered the pulmonary circulation of the blood, was sentenced to death by a founding father of Protestantism, John Calvin. **People with an untrained and unmanaged mind are so attached to their ego that they are their ego as far as they know.** As a result, rather than consider and try to understand others with opposing views of the world around them and update their ego, it is far more likely that they will feel anxiety and argue against opposing beliefs without any hesitation or consideration because the very existence of their mind feels under threat and in danger.

When you realize that your ego is merely one useful (all be it fallible) component of your mind that YOU control, and when you separate your inner-self from your ego, it gives you the freedom to observe and question everything about who you think you are, what you think you know about the world around you and actively question and research your own beliefs. **You will find that as you detach yourself from your ego and recognize it as an independent component of your mind, you will be able to evolve a truly open mind.** You will happily question all aspects of your ego without feeling threatened by the thought that what you believe to be true may not actually be so.

A fascinating fact is that most people acquire their beliefs from the environment in which they grow up. Their ego is, in fact, shaped by their parents, their friends, and the immediate society or community in which they grow up. A person's ego is often not based on any particular facts, education, or research. In fact, the brainwashing becomes so complete over time that an individual becomes convinced that their picture of themselves, their view of the world around them, and their beliefs are entirely true and will even make up sophisticated rationals that support their vision of them regardless of the facts, in the same way that the catholic church completely rejected the evidence presented to them by Galileo.

Exercise 5: Just for a moment, think about your own political or religious beliefs. Ask and answer these questions right now. Do you hold beliefs that you grew up with and acquired through your upbringing rather than through detailed research and analysis? Are your beliefs the same as your parents or closest friends? Have you genuinely allocated time to study alternative beliefs and compare them with your own? Have you considered that if you collaborated with others who hold different beliefs, there might be an even better truth awaiting you? Do you largely rely on leaps of faith rather than rational, intellectual analysis for any of your beliefs? **How far would you go to defend what you think is true about your current religious or political beliefs rather than collaborate to seek the ultimate truth or a better understanding or a better solution?**

Attachments are the root cause of stress and anxiety

As explained above, being attached to your mind, emotions, and ego can all lead to stress and anxiety. Separating the inner-you from your intellect, emotions, and ego gives you control of these and allows you to prevent jumping to conclusions and responding with knee-jerk reactions. In addition, your attachments to people, possessions, power, and wealth can also lead to stress and anxiety. For example, separating from a partner or the loss of a loved one can be devastating. However, it doesn't have to be. That is not to say that you have to become a cold, heartless individual to the extent that nothing phases you. It is more about learning how to put things into a proper context so that you do not have to experience long-term sadness or anxiety. Allowing grief to get a hold of you is similar to allowing anger to take control of you. Neither solves the problem nor changes the past. Neither benefits the future. Don't get me wrong, a short burst of sadness and a good cry can actually be beneficial. In the same way increasing your comfort levels or getting short bursts of pleasure are not bad as long as you do not let these things drive you. When you cry, the body releases endorphins that can actually make you feel better.

However, be aware, exaggerated expressions of grief or regret are technically selfish reactions, the same as anger. Grief manifests due to the negative impact that a person, thing, or happening you are grieving over will have on you. Here are some examples to demonstrate this point.

Imagine you are watching someone at a roulette table putting $10,000 on red. The wheel spins, and the number comes up black. The money is lost. You feel nothing at all. It's not your money. Now imagine that the person said they took the $10,000 from your bank account. You are probably now going to feel a combination of anger and grief. The only difference is that in the first instance, your mind did not have an attachment to the money. In the second instance, your mind did have an attachment to it, and you would feel bad because of the theft and the effect that losing $10,000 is going to have on you. If you are super rich, your attachment may not be that great, which may not bother you that much. If you are of average wealth, it will hurt you a lot more. It is all dependent on having an attachment and the degree of attachment.

Now imagine that you are reading in the newspaper that a person has lost their spouse or child in an accident. Sure, you may feel an element of sadness for them, but you will soon forget it and think nothing of it. It will not affect your happiness or cause you anxiety. However, what if it is your spouse or child. Because of the attachment you have and the impact this would have on your life, you would feel a great deal of grief, stress, and anxiety, even though these feelings cannot change the past or improve the outcomes of the future.

The same is true for any example you can think of. Whether it is watching someone else drop and smash their mobile phone or seeing your own mobile phone drop and smash. The more attached you are to people and things, the bigger the negative impact, the more these things can cause you grief, stress, and anxiety.

Many philosophies and religions recognize this and recommend something referred to as renunciation. Most people interpret this as giving up everything or giving everything away. Indeed, not owning things can lead to less stress. Not owning something releases you from any stresses related to owning that thing. For example, it could be the constant repair bills for an expensive car. No car, no repair bills. However, renunciation does not mean giving up all your relationships and possessions in order to achieve happiness.

What renunciation actually means is to learn how to give up your mental attachment to things. You do not have to actually give up the things themselves. You can still enjoy the things you own and love and enjoy the people around you, but understanding that pretty much everything in life is temporary, there is no value in grief when they are gone. Recognize the joy or pleasure you once experienced, or celebrate the love you once had and move forward. With certain things, it may be just temporary as you will simply replace the item. With other things, the loss may be permanent, and it is merely a matter of moving on with your life to the next set of experiences that come your way or that you seek out.

Without question, this is way harder than it sounds. It is human nature to form strong attachments to both things and people. It takes considerable experience and effort to simultaneously love and yet remain detached. It can only be achieved by understanding and practicing self-awareness, being present, using your intellect to put things into context, and ensuring you remain detached from your ego and emotions. However, with intellectual understanding and practice, it can be achieved.

Your Body

Where does your body fit into all of this?

In addition to being the container hosting your intellect, ego, and emotions, your body is also the location of your biological sensors, known as your five senses, which allow you to experience the world, i.e., sight, sound, smell, taste, and touch. It is also the mechanical equipment that gives you the ability to move, communicate, act, and react. **Quite simply, your senses are constantly monitoring what is going on around you. Your intellect interprets and considers these experiences, factoring in how your involuntary emotions make you feel and how your ego defines you and the world around you, and then instructs the body to act or react accordingly.** Regardless of the circumstance, our life is quite simply made up of a constant repetition of this process. If a bear starts running at you in the woods, you may decide to stand still and be silent. You may decide to run and scream. You may decide to pick up a large branch and start running and shouting at the bear. You choose how to react to what your senses are telling you. The more present, aware, detached, and knowledgeable you are, the better your decisions and actions will be.

Without your body, the process of living as described above is not possible. The better your health and general fitness, the better your body can perceive the world around you and operate within it. Many tradesmen learn early on, 'look after your tools, and your tools will look after you.'

Now What?

Don't overthink

If finding happiness from the inside rather than from external distractions and pleasures resonates with you and you decide to embark on a quest to experiment with the techniques outlined here, then be aware not to overthink and get too attached to the techniques themselves. It is not uncommon for people to understand and start letting go of their attachments to the people and things around them while remaining connected to them, but then find that they inadvertently get fully attached to the ideas and techniques of living the right way that their mind goes into another chatter loop obsessing over whether they have understood and are carrying out the techniques correctly, or wondering if they are making enough effort. Don't overthink it or overwork it. Let it take time, and let it happen naturally. None of the techniques in this book can be experienced by reading the words alone. Become self-aware, stop your mind chattering and feel what the words are trying to describe, the more you stop your mind chattering, and the more you feel what you learn, the faster you will arrive at your ultimate goal. At some point in time, you will no longer need the words, you will live effortlessly in a continuous lasting state of peace, pleasure, relaxation, and happiness.

Before moving on

By the time you have completed chapters 1 and 2, you should have achieved the following:

1. Recognized that the world around you is not able to provide you lasting happiness or a stress-free life. The world around you is merely the space where your body carries YOU around, with things happening around you and to you, much of which you have little or no control over. Attempting to control the things around you through wealth or power to achieve lasting happiness is naive, foolhardy, and can only manifest in certain and constant disappointment. Even if you are fortunate enough to experience extreme comfort and an array of short-term pleasures, on their own, they will never be enough.
2. Experienced first hand that you are not your mind. that your inner-self is pure consciousness and a separate entity that independently recognizes and senses all the functioning components that collectively make up who you are and that YOU, your inner-self, can control.
3. Learned some simple techniques to help you a) experience and become self-aware, b) to experience and become present, and c) to help you identify and remain independent of your intellect, ego, and emotions.
4. Learned a style of meditation that can help manage and dissipate your instinctive and involuntary emotions.
5. Learned and recognized that your attachment to people and things can frequently be the source of grief, stress, and anxiety.

If you feel that these objectives have not been met, have a slow re-read. The value of learning the art of living is greatly diminished without experiencing, recognizing, and understanding these things.

Chapter 3

The Importance of Education and Knowledge

Warning! Sections of this chapter may challenge your beliefs and perceptions of life. The intention is not to upset you or to ignite your ego into defending itself and your beliefs. It is intended to get your inner-you to engage your intellect and make you think. We all know people that are set in their ways, not prepared to learn new things or challenge their thoughts, beliefs, or ways of doing things. Does this describe you too? Please read this chapter with an open mind, stay present, aware and let the inner-you control your intellect, ego, and emotions rather than the other way around. The experience of letting go and opening your mind is empowering. Embrace it, don't fear it.

Why jumping to conclusions can be a problem

Jumping to conclusions is a human instinct. In the past, and in certain circumstances even today, we can find ourselves in a tricky situation where we need to assess the situation quickly in order to get clear. However, it is also one of humanity's most significant failings. Sometimes we get it right, but there are a good many times that we get it wrong and that can be bad!

The problem is we are only human and are just as likely to jump to the wrong conclusion as the right one as demonstrated by the following anecdote. One day an alien from a far distant planet visits Earth. He has been tasked with finding out one thing about our planet. He decides to visit a bar. On his first day of research, he drinks whiskey and soda and gets drunk. The next day he goes to the bar again and this time he drinks vodka and soda. Sure enough, he gets drunk again. On the final day of his mission, he goes to the bar and drinks gin and soda, again until drunk. The next day he immediately goes back to his home planet and prepares his report. His conclusion, soda gets you drunk.

This anecdote demonstrates how easy it can be to jump to the wrong conclusion when you do not have all the facts or information at your disposal. With many circumstances we try to judge on the spot, we often do not have all the information or knowledge required even though we sometimes think we do, or worse, have relied on someone else's word who may also not know even if they say they do. The more effort we make to gather the facts, evidence, and knowledge to make a sound conclusion the better. This is where education and knowledge come into their own.

The three perceptions of truth

At any given time, there are three perceptions of truth. In some cases, they may all be the same. In others, they may all be different. The first perception is the truth of the masses, i.e., the truth of a majority or a large group of people. The second perception is the truth of an individual or a small group. It may be the same as the truth of the majority, or it may oppose the majority. Then, there is truth itself, the ultimate truth. Back in Galileo's time, the mass truth, and that of the Church, was that the sun orbited the earth. Then there was an individual's or small group's truth. Galileo, together with other scientists, believed that the earth orbited the sun. Then there was the ultimate truth. In this example, Galileo was correct. The earth orbits the sun. These three perceptions of truth can be applied to many different examples. One of the biggest questions of all time still remains, how did our universe come about.

CHAPTER 3

For the most part, people automatically defend their own belief regardless of whether it is actually true or not. I am certain we are all aware of situations where we have defended what we believe rather than questioned what we believe.

Scientists as a community are typically trained to avoid forming strong beliefs. Instead, they create theories that they think might be true. It is then the practice of the science community collectively to challenge, research and study multiple theories to see if any one of these is, in fact, the ultimate truth. They need to remain open-minded enough to accept that any one of the theories could be the ultimate truth, regardless of its origin. Furthermore, they even remain open-minded enough to accept the discovery of a new additional alternative theory that turns out to be the ultimate truth. Sadly, this approach is not generally adopted in any other aspect of our lives. Unprepared and untrained **people are generally more concerned about defending their individual truths, especially if supported by a like-minded group of people, sometimes ready to inflict death and destruction rather than work collectively to discover the ultimate truth.** You only need to look at politics and religion to see this is the case.

How does this information help? **When you are in the observer state, i.e., present, aware, and independent of your intellect, emotions, and ego, it is remarkable the power this gives you in any given situation.** You no longer need to spontaneously react, get emotional or defend your ego. You can observe yourself and what is going on around you and give yourself time to consider what reaction you should give in order to obtain the best outcome in any given situation. It may even be little or no reaction at all. Perhaps you will even decide to walk away and consider conducting detailed research on the issue rather than respond. You may even be in a situation where you can collaborate with a person having an alternative point of view or belief and explore the question together to find the ultimate truth. In a nutshell, you place yourself in a position where you can observe. Control your emotions. Use your intellect to review and rationalize the situation, rather than letting your intellect control you into doing something you will regret, and then select the best reaction for the best outcome. It may even include re-evaluating and updating your views or beliefs. You should always be on the quest for the ultimate truth.

Ignorance is definitely not bliss

Knowledge is Power

People, especially groups of people of the same opinion, frequently allow their emotions and ego to prompt their intellect into acting upon, defending, or arguing for what they believe to be true, surprisingly often with little or no evidence. The big differentiator is knowledge. In the case of Galileo, his studies led to the knowledge that proved his conclusions were correct. His opponents did not even consider the possibility of reviewing his findings.

One man to fully understand that knowledge is power is Nathan Rothschild. Following twenty years of war after the French revolution between the French, British, and other allies, British bond prices on the stock market continually fluctuated up and down depending on the outcome of the various battles being fought at the time. At the Battle of Waterloo on June 18, 1815, a victory by Britain or its allies would send the bond prices soaring since it would reduce the risk of defeat, default, and more government borrowing. A defeat would send prices plummeting for opposite reasons. These conditions gave plenty of opportunity for market manipulation through the manufacture of fake battlefield news, given that information traveled at the speed of horses and sailing ships. Nathan Rothschild was fully aware of this and had established his own high-speed battlefield information infrastructure. He knew that he would need to know the outcome of battles before anyone else to stay ahead. As it turns out, other speculators knew that Rothschild was getting accurate information before anyone else too, and decided that all they needed to do was follow Rothschild's stock market moves. If Rothschild started buying British bonds, they would know that the British had won and that British stocks and bonds would rise. If he began to sell British bonds, then the Brits must have lost, they assumed.

CHAPTER 3

On the day of the battle, Rothschild quietly started to sell off British bonds in large numbers, banking the cash. This move became known by the other traders, which prompted a frenzy of speculators selling off British stocks, assuming that the British had lost the battle. The price of British bonds plummeted to rock bottom. When the prices went as low as possible, Rothschild took the cash he had taken out of the market when the bonds were high and bought all of the bonds at the bottom of the market. The news came in that the British had won, and the British bond prices sky-rocketed. Nathan Rothschild made a killing! The collective assets of the five Rothschild brothers in spring 1815 came to $750,000 (at a time when the average wage was about $75 per year); in July 1816, it was $1.5 million. Nathan Rothschild knew that speculators were following his moves and used that knowledge, together with the real news he had gathered, to manipulate the market in his favor.

I'm not proposing that the smart thing to do is acquire knowledge to manipulate others. The primary value of acquiring knowledge is to prevent yourself from being manipulated by others, which is a fundamental way to avoid landing in stressful circumstances. Making an effort to learn and gain a real understanding of the things that govern your life can be a game-changer, and with the internet at your disposal, it has never been easier. **Do not assume second-hand facts or information is reliable when reported by third parties like the media or known figures. Always question and do your own research.** There may be limits to what you find out. Do not make assumptions for the benefit of convenience or to support what you believe. Recognize that you do not have all the information you need and do not arrive at any conclusion. Keep an open mind. There are two important lessons to be gained from the Rothschild example. Rothschild knew that he would receive accurate news of the battle. He also knew that speculators would follow him. The speculators also knew that Rothschild would receive the news first, a known known. They did not factor in that Rothschild would manipulate the market. It was an unknown unknown.

Your reason for being

While I hope you can remain present, aware, and open-minded throughout reading this book, it is definitely a must for this section. Observe yourself, and what you are thinking, as you read this section.

Many believe they are put on Earth for a reason and that things happen for a reason. Why?

Where do people get the idea there is a reason for them to be here or a reason for things to happen? There is no evidence for this of any kind. It is nothing more than conjecture and cannot be substantiated through any evidence, rational thought, or verification. Just because you read it somewhere, or some adult told you this as a kid, or because you cannot think of another explanation. None of these are evidence. If it were true, if you are here for a reason or if things happen for a reason, how is it you don't know what the reason is? Isn't that a little pointless, to have a reason for being here and not know what that reason is? Wouldn't that just make you a simple stooge, carrying out some part in a plan you know nothing about? More than that, it is highly improbable. On close examination, it just doesn't add up. However, it does reinforce the proposition that **we are prone to jumping to conclusions and accept explanations without consideration, research, or verification**. We see it all the time.

While jumping to conclusions can give short-term satisfaction and help settle the uneducated and untrained mind, at best, it is only a short-term pacifier and not a route to lasting happiness. At worst, it is dangerous and can lead to extreme unhappiness, significant unrest, endanger lives and even cause death. You only have to observe the impact of fake news to see this is true. The storming of the US Capitol on January 6th, 2021, is just one example of how blind belief can be dangerous. People lost their lives, and they really should not have had to. History is littered with similar examples.

The world is full of people ready to take lies presented as truth or handed down beliefs at face value without proper consideration or verification. Either because it satisfies a narrative they support, or they want to fit in with a particular crowd, or they just can't be bothered to employ their intellect (or don't know how). It is known as herd stupidity fueled by blind faith or blind belief. Do not believe anything based on blind faith; remain skeptical and open-minded on all matters until you have indisputable evidence and can verify things for yourself. Until that point, you do not know.

A more pragmatic and intellectual approach is to recognize and accept that we do not know or understand as much of the world around us as we think. We can still learn to find lasting happiness and live in peace. For example, most of us do not know the complete list of the components in our TV or how they work. But that does not prevent us from turning on the TV and enjoying our favorite TV show.

Whether you think there is a reason for us to be here or not makes no difference in how life happens. Your life will still be filled with a stream of things going on all around you. Why? Not for any particular reason we will ever be able to discover, other than the fact that all events that take place in the universe are the current reaction to a chain of events that started when all that exists came to be. On this particular subject, we do not need to know more than this to live a fulfilling, happy life. There are so many more things in the world out there to discover that can have a positive effect on your life.

The joy of learning

The word Education is derived from the Latin educatum, which means "to lead out." That is to say, education means to lead out or bring out the internal talents of a child or person. Education does not mean learning and remembering a collection of facts. A person needs to develop understanding within, which when required can be supported by facts.

A reporter once interviewed Albert Einstein for an article. At the end of the interview, the reporter asked for Einstein's number to call if he had more questions. "Of course," said Einstein. He picked up the phone book, looked up his phone number, wrote it on a piece of paper, and handed it over. Surprised, the reporter said, "You are considered to be the smartest man in the world, and you can't remember your own phone number?" "No," Einstein replied.

"Why should I memorize something I can easily get from a book?"

Consider teaching math to a young child who does not know mathematics. You could quite quickly teach them that 2+2 = 4. When asked the question, what is 2+2, the child can easily remember to say 4. If you then ask what 45+372 is, they would not know the answer. Mathematics requires understanding. You need to learn numbers, what they are, and what they represent. Once you understand numbers, you recognize any put in front of you. Furthermore, you also need to learn what the + symbol is and does. Once you have this understanding, you can add up any two numbers put in front of you. This is true in all areas of learning. It **is important to evolve an understanding from within, not just memorize the words**.

An interesting observation is that obtaining a degree does not in itself give rise to talent or success. For example, Shakespeare did not attend university to learn how to write, yet he is considered one of the greatest writers of all time. Yet many go to university to study his work. **Ironically, going to university to study Shakespeare and a whole host of other great writers, many of whom did not go to university, does not mean you obtain your degree with the ability to write like Shakespeare or any other writer. You have to spend time bringing out your own talent from within**.

Needing to evolve one's own understanding of life is especially important when learning and practicing the art of living. For example, we all grow up being taught the difference between good and bad, but quite frequently, some anomalies can confuse us and lead us to the wrong conclusions. For example, we know that lying is bad. Lying to one's partner, lying to one's friends, etc., is considered very anti-social and potentially harmful in some form or another. When we are kids, our parents distinctly tell us that lying is bad and we should never do it. Then around the same time, they tell us that Santa Clause, the Tooth Fairy, and the Easter Bunny all exist! What message does this send, what do we learn from this. That lying is acceptable under certain circumstances. If so, what are those circumstances and who gets to draw the line, and what if that line is drawn differently between two people in a relationship or doing business together? **Deep conscious understanding changes everything**.

Learning facts is relatively easy, and it merely requires a good memory.

Developing an understanding takes time and much more effort. You need to learn each step and fully understand it before moving on to the next. Initially, it can be a chore; the effort involved is significant. Over time it becomes easier as you experience the rewards. The more you read and practice, the more you understand. Progressively, you will develop sufficient understanding to confront any situation and continue to live a lasting happy, and stress-free life.

Education is a wonderful thing.

A note on the word enlightenment

Language too is a wonderful thing. The ability for people to communicate through words is an amazing development of humanity. However, there are limitations with communicating with words, as we have seen in examples given earlier when trying to describe feelings or flavors. Learning from words alone rarely offers a complete way to develop a skill. Imagine learning to swim, drive a car, or play the piano merely by reading a book. A book may give you a rudimentary theoretical overview, and you may have a clear understanding of the words, but that will not provide a complete understanding of its practical application. The learning process can only be completed with practical exercises. This is even more true when trying to communicate philosophical concepts where words can have multiple interpretations depending on the writer's and reader's differing backgrounds.

Words like God, Spirituality Enlightened, and Enlightenment have all come to mean different things for different people. Conjuring up different understandings and interpretations. As far as the word enlightenment is concerned, the origin of the word represents the best definition. It is from Middle English simply describing the action 'to make luminous'; 'to shine.' In other words, 'to remove blindness or 'to shine a light on.' It can be used in any situation where someone learns something new, becoming both aware of and fully understands what is new to them.

In the context of learning to live in a way that enables you to achieve lasting happiness and live a completely stress-free life, enlightenment is simply when you are a) aware of how to live the right way, b) when you fully understand the words and their true significance, c) when you can experience and verify what you learned for yourself, and d) when you put into practice what you have learned.

In the context of this book, it means when you can remain self-aware and present at all times. When you fully understand all the guidelines and concepts. And when you have developed the skills and employ them in your everyday living.

Intellect vs. intelligence vs. intellectual

The intellect is that part of the mind that takes in information, then reasons and rationalizes. It is the voice inside your mind that chatters and tries to make sense of what is going on around you. By default, it tends to jump to conclusions. Nevertheless, it is a powerful tool when controlled by the inner-self.

Intelligence is the level of capability individuals have in being able to rationalize and reason. Some people are naturally brilliant and find it easy to rationalize and reason arriving at pretty reliable conclusions off the bat. They are more likely not to jump to conclusions too early. They review all information and knowledge at their disposal, conduct research, and arrive at an informed judgment rather than jumping to a conclusion. Others are less intelligent. They are either too lazy or find it harder to reason and often jump to conclusions early rather than think things through. One point of note here, intelligence is also dependent on education. Intelligent people can also arrive at dumb conclusions if they are based on false knowledge that they think they know to be true. **The ego, too, can cloud the mind of even the most intelligent. In general, intelligent people are more likely to rationalize and reason and are more prepared to question even what they think to be true.**

An intellectual is a person who spends time building their intellect and intelligence through constant study and the quest for knowledge. Separating the inner-you from your intellect and ego gives you the ability to direct your mind toward increasing intellect and intelligence. It is a worthy pursuit as we discuss in more detail in the next chapter.

The process of learning

Moving from the known to discover what is currently unknown is **similar to switching on your car's headlights when you go for a long drive at night. The headlights do not illuminate your whole journey; they only illuminate what is immediately in front of you. As you move forward, the light reveals more to you and enables you to travel the full length of your journey.** The most effective way to learn is to study, verify, reflect, practice, and repeat. Each element of knowledge you acquire for yourself replaces an element of ignorance. Keep moving forward, and you will arrive at your ultimate goal.

Having the right mindset when it comes to knowledge

Keeping your ego in check.

As noted by Donald Rumsfeld, there are three knowns, **"There are known knowns. These are things we know that we know. There are known unknowns. That is to say, there are things that we know we don't know. But there are also unknown unknowns. The things we don't know we don't know."**

It is remarkable the number of people that assume that they know. Especially if they have grown up with certain beliefs fully supported by the people and community around them. However, for the sake of protecting yourself from your intellect and your ego, it is better to operate with a more open mind. We behave far less arrogantly when working on the basis that **there are <u>assumed</u> knowns rather than known knowns. That being the things we <u>think</u> we** know rather than know we know. And to consider there are the <u>assumed</u> **unknowns. That is to say, there are things that we <u>think</u> we don't know. And of course, there are the unknown unknowns, the ones that catch us all by surprise unless we are mentally prepared.** Being self-aware, observing ourselves and the people around us as life unfolds, recognizing that what we think we know may not be so, and making every effort to constantly learn and verify our knowledge with first-hand facts and experiences significantly increases our ability to reason and our increases our intelligence. Constantly learning is good. It helps us evolve.

Too be (smart) or not to be - The choice is yours

Intelligence without education is like a powerful computer without software or data. There has never been a better time in history to educate yourself. As the saying goes,

> *"If you don't want to be educated, no one can help you. If you do want to be educated, no one can stop you."*

There is no question that constantly improving your education, especially in areas you enjoy or that affect you on a day-to-day basis, brings both pleasure and reward.

Ten steps to learning the art of living and becoming 'enlightened.'

As with learning any art, there is a logical sequence of steps that help you learn faster. With the piano, you start with finger exercises and practicing scales. When learning to swim, you start in shallow water, learning to float and propel yourself with your arms and legs. When learning to ride a bike, you learn how to balance and push yourself off to get going. Learning the art of living, leading to lasting happiness, is no different. **The key steps are as**

follows:

1. Experience and practice self-awareness.
2. Learn techniques to remain self-aware and control your chattering mind whenever possible.
3. Experience and practice being fully present.
4. Practice and remain independent of your intellect, ego, and emotions.
5. Study and understand what makes up your experiences as you experience them through each of your senses.
6. Re-evaluate your relationship with the world and your experiences. Increase your ability to realistically interpret your experiences before labeling and reacting to them. Do not judge or knee-jerk-react to your experiences.
7. Learn to be connected and yet detached from all things. Practice this form of renunciation.
8. Use meditation and breathing techniques to prevent negative emotions from controlling you, heighten your self-awareness, and keep your mind in the present moment.
9. Learn the art of living.
10. Use and manage your body and mind to good effect. That is to say, formulate your own purpose in life.

How much learning is required?

This is a question only you can answer as you progress. With the basics in place, some will have enough information to get the ball rolling and progressively develop a complete understanding leading to full enlightenment quite quickly, learning by themselves as they assess themselves and how they react to their experiences and what is going on around them. For others, and likely most, it may take longer and may require more help. For some, it can take much of their life. There is a lovely line in the first Superman movie with Christopher

Reeves and Gene Hackman. Lex Luther is expressing frustration with the slow wit of his associate and says,

> "Some people can read War and Peace and come away thinking it's a simple adventure story. Others can read the ingredients on a chewing gum wrapper and unlock the secrets of the universe."

We are all different and learn different things at different speeds, and that's fine. **Learn at your own pace**.

There are other factors too that will influence how much learning you think you will need. For example, **if you live a content life and are experiencing relatively low-stress levels, you may feel you are happy enough and do not need to learn more to be happy. On the other hand, if you feel that you are in a bad place and that the world is conspiring against you, you may want to allocate a considerable amount of time to learn and understand**. Necessity is not only the mother of invention; it is also a catalyst for learning.

Another factor will be determined by what extent you want to become enlightened. **Enlightenment is not an on or off proposition.** There is a scale from zero to one hundred. Many people will have no interest or just cannot be bothered, representing a zero level of enlightenment, while one hundred percent represents a fully enlightened individual. Some of us may achieve complete enlightenment and live in a state of lasting bliss; others may simply learn enough to eliminate stress and live a good and happy life.

As mentioned earlier, the choice is yours.

Support the education and growth of others

When you begin to reduce your stress and become happier, people around you experiencing sadness and stress will stand out far more than you ever noticed before. In some circumstances, you may even find that this can impact you negatively, particularly if it is someone close to you. The simple answer is to help them grow too. Share what you have learned with them and encourage them as they develop. It is a classic example of a win-win.

4

Chapter 4

The Art of Living

This chapter has one primary objective, to provide an introduction to learning the art of living. For a person who can live life present, aware and detached, most of it is common sense, and you probably already know much of it. Many spiritual, religious, and philosophical texts provide a guide to living the right way. The Bible, the Koran, the Buddhavacana, the Upanishads, etc. Between them, they contain rules, anecdotes, and parables, among other things, that guide you to living a good life. The problem is that unless you are present, aware, and detached, you will continue to be managed by your mind and merely react to the events around you.

The following chapter is not intended to provide a set of rules to follow in the way that philosophical or religious texts do. It is intended to provide food for thought and stimulate your intellect into working it all out for yourself. It is a collection of concepts, ideas, and observations for you to consider and make sense of so that you can devise your own principles for living the right way based on your own experiences.

Prevention is better than cure

Living life within the Regret Minimization Framework - Derived from a quote made by Jeff Bezos.

For all intents and purposes, the vast majority of people sleepwalk through their lives allowing their untrained and unmanaged minds to be in control, moving from one experience to the next, chasing imaginary pots of gold at the end of hypothetical rainbows.

While remaining present, aware, and detached, the inner-you can have more control over how you feel and react to things going on around you. **Complete understanding comes when you also learn to live the right way in addition.**

The present is the past of the future. **By living the right way in the present, you can prevent yourself from inadvertently creating a regretful past**, eliminating the need for your intellect to spend unnecessary time regretting, stressing, or worrying about the past or obsessing over things that may or may not happen in the future.

Acquiring the art of living is simply learning, understanding, and practicing a collection of techniques for how to live your life in a way that minimizes stress and anxiety before the need to experience them. As demonstrated in a couple of examples in previous chapters, when your mind controls you, you are prone to knee-jerk reactions to the things going on around you that can often end up causing you even more grief and anxiety than you were experiencing in the first place. **Living life the right way can prevent unwanted unhappy, stressful outcomes from ever coming about in the first place.** Prevention is better than cure.

While Jeff Bezos does not come across as a particularly wise individual, one thing he said in an interview explaining how he came up with the 'Regret Minimization Framework' to help him decide if he should start Amazon or not was quite insightful. By identifying the least regretful outcome when he reached 80, he could determine what decision he should make in the present. Jeff decided that if he started Amazon and succeeded, he clearly would not regret this. He also determined that if he started Amazon and failed, he would not regret this either. At least he tried. He also knew that if he did not start Amazon, he would never know either way and regret not having tried. It would always be on his mind. Therefore, the decision to start Amazon essentially made itself. Make every decision with the Regret Minimization Framework in mind. (Link to interview https://youtu.be/jwG_qR6XmDQ)

Coming to terms with the world YOU live In

We all live in different worlds determined by where we are and what is going on around us. It's easy to say that money and possessions are not important. However, if you try walking out of a store with a basket full of groceries explaining to the cashier that you are enlightened and money is not important, you are definitely going to get a strange look, and you are definitely not going to be walking out of that store with any groceries.

Whether the world should be or could be a better place is a matter for debate, and in relation to having to live day-to-day in the world as it is, it is irrelevant. We live in the world as it is, and we have to operate within the environment we find ourselves in. The key is to develop your intelligence and enable your intellect to adapt what you increasingly learn and understand on your path to enlightenment in a way that allows you to live a stress-free and happy life within the environment in which you live. That does not mean that you should put up with your circumstances and learn to live with them or get used to them, not at all. **Accept your circumstances for what they are. Rather than allow your mind to constantly chatter in a loop stressing about the situation you are in or allowing desires to build up into monsters, the smart move is to sit down and prepare a plan to improve your circumstances. It is not bad or wrong to Improve your comfort levels and spend time on short-term pleasures, as long as you do not allow unattainable desires to form, build up and take over your life.** Wanting something that improves the comfort of your life or gives you a short-term burst of pleasure is very different from dwelling on desires and obsessing over things you cannot have at any given moment.

Everyone's circumstances are different, making it impossible to recommend a single course of action to suit all. You have to find your own path, learn and develop the art of living, and apply what you learn to your circumstances. You may be born into a rich or poor country, a rich or poor neighborhood, a rich or a low-income family. You do not get to choose the environment or circumstances in which you are born. Many other elements also have a massive impact on the circumstances you are born into. Who your parents are, what they do, their levels of intelligence and intellect, etc. It is no one's fault. There is no one to blame. It just is what it is. Rather than dwell on the unfairness of it all, or look for someone to blame, it is far more satisfying and productive to accept what is and plan your path to a better environment.

In general, it's fair to say that the better the environment you are born into, the more comfortable you are likely to be, and the more pleasures you are likely to experience. However, this does not guarantee a lasting stress-free, happy life, and only you can make that happen whatever the circumstances in which you live.

People born into poor environments are more likely to wish they could be rich, believing it will make them happy. Of course, it would bring additional pleasures and comfort for a short time until the next set of desires kick in and so on. (By the way, regardless of the level of wealth, most people would like to have more!) By contrast, some rich people may wish for a simpler, less complex life believing that this will make them happier. This desire, too, will only be short-lived. These are classic examples of the 'grass is always greener' syndrome. **Allocate time to understand the environment you are in. Accept and accommodate it for what it is.** Then list the different ways you can improve your life. Prepare a plan, then methodically and consistently work your plan, adjusting it along the way as circumstances around you change or as your thoughts evolve. There is nothing wrong with improving your life so long as your quest does not control or consume you.

Why do our intellects go on endless chatter loops?

Another natural human process is complex problem-solving. Some do it better than others, especially those that allocate time to educate themselves, and most importantly, develop their intellect. That aside, it is a natural process we all possess. When our lives are not going well, or we need to achieve something, our intellect automatically steps in and tries to work it out. Unfortunately, we have limitations. **Our minds can only think about and retain so many moves ahead at a time.** Chess masters, for example, can think many moves ahead when it comes to chess, but for most of us, and when it comes to day-to-day living, solving complex problems in our heads is a challenge. As we start to think through a problem and as we define the problem, we start to consider a variety of what-ifs and review a variety of factors that might impact various outcomes. We very quickly reach the capacity of our minds ability to store all the variables logically and helpfully. As a result, our intellect becomes overloaded and starts chattering around in circles with no resolution. The best way to break the loop however is quite simple. 1. Stop your mind chattering by making yourself present and aware. 2. Get out your preferred means of making notes. A pen and paper, a computer or tablet, it doesn't matter. 3. Start putting all that is chattering around in your mind down in a logical way that will allow you to define the problem. 4. Prepare a list of possible solutions, and 5. Develop a plan for moving forward. Get help if needed. A problem shared is a problem halved. Writing down what your intellect is chattering about and preparing plans for moving forward is a great way to remove clutter from your mind and make it easier for you to remain present, aware, and relaxed. It's similar to the comment Einstein made with his phone number in that there is no need to carry (and obsess over) information in your head if you have written it down and turned it into a solid plan.

The Importance of accepting what is

CHAPTER 4

Avoid unnecessary actions or reactions to what goes on around you.

A fundamental principle to remember at all times is the value of accepting what is. One of the biggest causes of sadness, stress, or anxiety is that our Intellect, ego, and emotions find it hard to process bad or catastrophic experiences. The untrained mind has a default primal process for dealing with bad or catastrophic events known as the five stages of grief, which was introduced to the world in the 1969 book On Death and Dying by Elisabeth Kübler-Ross. The five states are 1. Denial, 2. Anger, 3. Bargaining, 4. Depression and 5. Acceptance.

Denial is where the intellect is initially unable to process the event—not believing that perhaps a partner has decided to leave them, or that they have lost their job, or that they have lost a large sum of money. Typically, initial reactions to a catastrophic event resulting from denial are driven by our unmanaged emotions, ego, and intellect working in overdrive. Reactions include thinking the event did not happen or was a mistake or that somehow the event can be reversed in some way, even if deep down the person knows this is not the case.

Anger comes next, perhaps anger directed at a person they think is responsible, or at an object that caused the event, or perhaps at themselves for not foreseeing or preventing it. As noted earlier, Anger never adds value to any situation and is frequently destructive. More often than not, it makes situations even worse, not better.

Then comes bargaining, perhaps with a higher power promising to be good or take some action if the event is reversed or if the outcomes are improved. Or bargaining with a person that could reverse the event, e.g., promising to change if a partner agrees to take them back.

Depression follows once it has been determined that the event cannot or will not be reversed, people can become very depressed and stressed, perhaps believing that their life will never be the same again or get any better, or that they are, in fact, the ones at fault. This is particularly the case when losing a loved one or even your job. Many people suffer depression after such life-changing incidents.

Finally comes acceptance. Once the depression passes, it is understood that nothing can be done to reverse the event. Think back on your own life and consider any significant losses you have experienced and compare how you feel about them now to how you felt about them at the time.

Interestingly, while the five stages of grief are generally applied to significant life-changing events such as the loss of a loved one, a similar, all be it a less intense sequence of stages can apply with any bad experience, even relatively small ones. Here's an example of how a seemingly minor event can trigger a mini version of the five stages.

In an episode of Oprah many years ago, Oprah ran a test. One of Oprah's floor managers randomly selected people coming into the theater to watch the show and told them there had been a mix-up with their tickets and that they would not be able to come in to see the show. People reacted in very different ways. One particular couple, two friends that had wanted to see the show together, were selected. One of the women immediately went into a mini version of denial, explaining that this could not be possible because she had bought the tickets plenty of time in advance. She demonstrated anger at the fact that this mix-up had taken place and started explaining all of the reasons why she should be allowed in, leading to bargaining to see what she could do to get in. Of course, she would have gone home and been upset and depressed before finally getting past it and arriving at full acceptance. Her friend, on the other hand, reacted very differently. She immediately accepted that there was an issue. The friend calmly tried to discuss the matter with the floor manager to find out her options for moving forward—perhaps rescheduling for a future date or getting a return on her tickets. She took a completely different approach to her friend. She accepted the situation and moved straight into finding out the best and least stressful way of moving forward.

A thoroughly trained and enlightened mind will immediately acknowledge that an event has happened once it has happened. The individual may initially make a few rational checks to be sure. However, when an event takes place, there is immediate acceptance. There is no denial; there is no anger because the enlightened mind accepts things as they are and sees no value in denial or anger under any circumstance. There is no bargaining as there is an instant appreciation of what has happened and what action needs to be taken to move forward productively. There is no depression as the enlightened mind recognizes that bad things happen, and it's better to just deal with the situation and move on. **An enlightened mind does not react badly to negative experiences. The intellect guides the body to act positively and productively to move forward without stress or anxiety.**

Time heals all wounds

As noted earlier, allowing your mind to dwell on the past or the future is an unhelpful distraction. That said, understanding the power of time, developing your capacity for patience, and recognizing that most day-to-day challenges that lead to stress and anxiety can be resolved over time and can help prevent stress from building up in the first place.

In our high-speed, instant-gratification world, we can apply the same mindset to resolving problems and challenges. Whether we are calling a customer service line, fixing a car, mending a phone, making up with a friend, whatever it is, we tend to want problems to be resolved instantly, and when that can't happen, it can lead to stress, worry, and anxiety. In these instances, you can use your intellect to reshape your thinking and be aware that your problem will get to the point of resolution (one way or the other) at some point in time. While having problems solved instantaneously is always lovely, and if you see a simple, stress-free way to resolve your issue quickly, of course, you should take it. For those problems you cannot solve on the spot, use your intellect to set an approximate date or time when you think you might be able to solve the problem, steadily work towards a resolution, and de-stress.

Develop your capacity to be patient. Patience is more than a virtue, it's also a simple way to reduce stress and anxiety.

When is good or bad, right or wrong, just different?

In one of the examples given earlier, Galileo was right, so there are clearly instances where right and wrong exist. However, **when you travel the world, learn about and experience different cultures, you find it remarkable how both similar and yet very different people can be at the same time.** Quite frequently, the root of the differences between people is cultural. For example, Hindus revere cows and choose not to eat them. As a result of their upbringing, it genuinely upsets them. And yet, in most other countries, beef is considered a staple food item. Jews and Muslims, on the other hand, do not eat pork. The thought of it repulses them, and yet, pork in most other countries is considered delicious. The French eat horse meat, yet culturally in the US, eating horse meat is deemed disgusting. Dogs are considered delicious in Asia and even in Sweden, but most other cultures around the world find that distressing. **Who gets to decide who is right or wrong?** Or should we just acknowledge that there are different cultures and that every culture has the right to their preferred practices, the same as you do yours?

Differences exist in all aspects of our daily lives. Some people like Classical music, others Country, others Pop. When it comes to different people's tastes and preferences, there is often no right or wrong, good or bad; there is just different. Before labeling something good or bad, right or wrong, just because that is what your ego tells you and has chosen to accept, consider the possibility that it may just be different. See if it makes a difference to your state of mind.

CHAPTER 4

Analyzing and understanding your motives

We are all brought up being told that killing a person is wrong. For example, if a person goes to a school and starts killing students with a semi-automatic weapon, we all recognize that this is without any doubt a bad act. But let's say that one of the teachers has a pistol and shoots the person with the weapon preventing them from shooting any more students. Then we would all agree that killing the shooter was, in fact, a good act. By this demonstration, killing in itself is neither good nor bad. It is generally the case with most of the actions we take on a day-to-day basis. The context, motivation, and intention behind any act determine whether it is good or bad. A powerful technique for preventing regret is to thoroughly analyze your motivations and intentions for all your actions before you act. By remaining present and aware and observing yourself, you give your intellect a far better opportunity to review all that is going on around you and what is going on in your mind. It gives you the power to take entirely good actions. **As you develop the art of living, you will find that there is never a need to act with harmful intentions. There is always a better way.**

Why does giving into desires only lead to short-term pleasures?

While there are several reasons why giving in to desires leads to temporary pleasures, and indeed, in some cases leads to grief and sadness. One significant reason to be aware of is that **desires are often based on illusory perceptions of the happiness that the desire in question is expected to bring, without considering any of the downsides.** Our intellect rarely factors in the whole story. Very often, the reality of owning an item or being with a particular person is very different from the perception of this item or person when it was a desire. Desires tend to be an exaggeration of the perceived pleasure as the mind purely focuses on the upsides. Desires invariably come with a downside and, in some cases, even a whole bunch of **unintended consequences**. As the expression goes,

"Be careful what you wish for, you may just get it."

Desires evolve from the emptiness you experience not being present and aware. Your intellect recognizes that something is missing, but it doesn't know what it is. As a result, your mind tries to work out how to fill the void, crudely determining that if things or people can provide short-term pleasures, then having more will increase the amount and frequency of those pleasures leading to lasting happiness. The problem is, it just doesn't work out that way. The more you get, the shorter the pleasures become as you become numb to their effect and the more you want. It is a vicious circle that never ends.

As a self-aware and present person, you can disconnect from and reshape your ego, manage your emotions and intellect and eliminate desires of any kind. Understanding that people or things do not lead to lasting happiness should not stop you from enjoying relationships with people or enjoying experiences. Nor stop buying something that will bring joy to your life or add convenience or comfort. However, life gets so much better when you realize **people and things cannot provide lasting happiness. Only you, through becoming present, aware, detached, and practicing the art of living the right way can achieve happiness.**

Giving really is better than receiving

Two actions primarily drive our activity in society. Giving and taking. If a society is predominantly driven by taking, this generates an environment dominated by selfish demands and desires and puts society in conflict and stress. **If everyone is driven by the need to take, where does the giving come from?**

The well-known phrase, giving is better than receiving, is barely understood by the majority of people. Yes, **we all know what the words mean, and we all recognize that giving something to someone also rewards us with a short-term feeling of pleasure. Despite knowing this, many people operate with a mindset of taking before giving.**

As you start to realize that the things you once desired only provide short-term pleasures, and as you become more aware and live life in the present, you will notice that your actions start to develop a greater spirit of giving. You become inclined to serve rather than take without the need to receive something in return. As you practice the art of living, there becomes progressively less need for you to spend time taking from the world around you. This reduced desire to acquire things to make you happy starts to evolve naturally as you become more regularly present, aware and detached. You don't need to force it. As you increasingly develop a desire to give and serve, you will find this infiltrates every aspect of your life. At home, with friends, at work, and even with strangers. You will then find yourself in the position where you want to give and serve more, a process that, ironically over time, starts to provide all manner of rewards that you never imagined possible. At this point, you will truly understand the saying giving is better than receiving.

Be aware that it does not happen overnight, and you should not force it. It is just something that evolves as you start to live life the right way.

Something else to note, like the true meaning of renunciation, **giving does not mean handing out all of your available cash and possessions**. While some have chosen to renounce everything to achieve enlightenment, it is not essential to become enlightened. There is nothing wrong with living a comfortable life or experiencing short-term pleasures, so long as the desire to do so does not take over your life.

Furthermore, There are many ways to give; it's just a matter of finding what works best for you. You can also give your time to help and support others, and you can also give your knowledge and experience to develop and encourage others.

Give consideration to your acts of kindness

It is important to differentiate between naive acts of kindness and fruitful acts of kindness. The latter requires the application of intellect. Taking the old proverb,

"If you give a man a fish, he can eat for a day. If you teach a man to fish, he can eat for a lifetime,"

we can highlight the difference. If you see a starving person and give them food each day, this person becomes dependent on you and a burden to you and others. On the surface, it seems as if you are being kind. In fact, you are perpetuating the problem. If you assist that person in providing food for themselves, then your genuine kindness removes any burden on you, and you provide a lasting solution for the person you have helped. Think about the things you can do for your community or the people around you to help find lasting solutions to the problems the people in your community face.

Should you care what people think about you?

Many people worry about what others think of them. It could be their boss, their partner, their friends or neighbors, any number of people. They feel they have to serve others and remain in a good light in the minds of others. On the surface, modifying your behavior to try and put yourself in a good light or to impress or avoid hurting others seems as if you are making life better for them or better for yourself. **Modifying your behavior to impact what others may think of you is a form of deceit and, most often, a burden.** Such behavior gives rise to stress and anxiety. More frequently than not, one way or another, it backfires. In the words of William Shakespeare, from Act 1, Scene III of the famous play hamlet, Polonius says:

*"This above all: **to thine own self be true.**"*

It does not mean that you should be selfish or cruel to others for the benefit of yourself. **With kindness underlying all your actions and reactions, even if on occasion you need to be cruel to be kind, you will experience peace, calm, and joy,** regardless of what others may think of you, as long as your actions are taken with the right motives and intentions.

CHAPTER 4

Why do so many evil people succeed?

As the old saying goes,

> "All that evil needs to succeed is for good people to do nothing."

There are countless examples of people witnessing wrong-doing and doing nothing to stop it or prevent it. In general, only a few react against bad or evil, sometimes at a high cost to themselves. There is more to this than meets the eye, and it goes beyond there being just good people and bad people in the world. There are four types of people: The aggressively good, the aggressively bad, the passively good, and the passively bad.

The aggressively good are those that live their life knowingly and actively for good. They make an active effort to contribute to society, and they, too, are the ones that actively fight against evil or injustice.

The aggressively bad actively act only in their own best interests and have no regard for others unless it serves their purpose. They will even quite happily harm others if it means getting what they want. Many in this category are identified as sociopaths or psychopaths.

The passively good, the majority, are the ones that generally live a good life but do not actively seek to go out and make the world a better place. Nor do they make an effort to step in when they see evil. These are the good people that allow evil to succeed.

The passively bad individuals are the ones that seek to look after their own best interests and are ready to see harm done to others, even if they do not actively go out to harm others. These people also look the other way when they see others do harm, they may even assist.

It's little wonder then when you think about it, with only one group of people acting in an aggressively good way, evil has every chance of success. **The more enlightened you become, the more you will become an aggressively good person, and you will stand out as a beacon for others to admire and follow.**

Understanding and managing expectations

Another simple way to reduce stress quickly is to lower your expectations of people. It's not hard, it just requires a little conscious effort. That doesn't mean you have to reduce your standards but don't assume that other people have the same standards as you or want to do things the way you do. Simply put. The higher your expectations are of people, the greater the likelihood that they will not meet your expectations. In turn, this means that you will more likely be disappointed, or in your view, let down by them, which will cause you more stress and anxiety and will probably put a strain on your relationship with that person.

Try resetting your mindset and see if it can reduce your stress. Expect nothing from anyone. If you give someone a task and they let you down. No big deal, you were not expecting anything. If they deliver a mediocre job, then it's not a complete disaster, and if they deliver an exceptional job, you're way ahead. When you set arbitrary benchmarks on how people should behave or perform based on your standards, the likelihood of being let down is much higher. If you start your expectations low and assume that people will not meet your standards, then it can only go up from there.

Furthermore, if people do end up falling short of your standards, you can view it more as an opportunity to help. You can work with that person in a non-condescending way to help them become aware of your standards, explain why these standards are important, and teach them how to achieve the standards you are looking for. In this way, not only do you not get frustrated by any person not meeting your standards in the first instance, but you also get to provide positive encouragement to someone and help them grow into being better. It's a win-win.

CHAPTER 4

A simple way to improve your life immediately

Look for the best in all people

In addition to reducing your expectations of people, you can quite simply go one step further to improve your relationship with the world and people around you. With just this small shift in attitude, **when you look for the good in people rather than focus on the bad, you will find the world becomes a significantly better place to live.** We all have our faults, we all have off days, we all make mistakes. As you become more self-aware and live more in the present, you will notice how many people around you do not. As you observe yourself, you will also naturally observe the people around you and interact with you. You will become increasingly aware that many, perhaps even most or even all of the people around you are not self-aware and allow their minds and emotions to control them rather than the other way around. Do not judge or criticize. To focus on the worst and react negatively degrades and diminishes your own state. Your ego will define others as lesser than you, your intellect will start to consider yourself better than others, and you may begin to experience emotions of anger or superiority. Suddenly you will find your mind is again controlling YOU. Remember that everyone's inner self is the same as yours, pure consciousness.

Exercise 6: If you are not already present and aware (because you are so engrossed in this book, for example!), take a moment to put yourself in that state now. Pause for a moment and stop the chattering of your intellect. Without using words in your mind, think of people you know. **With practice, you will sense that the inner-you is aware of the people you are thinking about. However, with the inner-you being just pure consciousness, it is not making any judgment or views of the people you are visioning in your mind.** If you start to think about the people you are visioning, perhaps some you love, some you admire, maybe some you do not like, what you begin to recognize is that there is a distinct separation between the inner-you being merely conscious and aware and your intellect, the part of you which attaches feelings, judgments and attributes to the people you know based on your experiences with these people and what you think you know about them. The picture you are building is what gets stored in your ego.

Have you ever witnessed a situation where an interaction has taken place between two strangers, and for one momentary slip-up, one person refers to the other as dumb or something similar? Take the example of a person buying ice cream in a shop. The customer requests one particular topping, and the server inadvertently puts on something different. With no knowledge of this person, apart from this one instance, the customer concludes that the server is dumb. There are several things to consider here. The server may be tired and more prone than usual to making mistakes at the end of their shift. They may have stresses or worries that are distracting them, making them operate below par. In fact, there may be any number of reasons for this error, including just being human. Have you ever made a silly mistake?

By not making a judgment, recognizing that you really do not know this person, understanding the server is likely not a bad person, realizing it was a mistake not deliberate, and further recognizing that the person is most likely not present and aware, the enlightened person will not react or think badly of this person. They will merely guide the person to getting the order right gently and calmly without fuss and without judgment.

The inner-you recognizes that people are who they are and accepts 'what is.' We are all the product of our upbringing and experiences. It is actually not the fault of any individual for being who they are until the point at which they become fully present and aware and can take charge of their lives and actions. When you recognize that people have just arrived at being who they are without engaging their consciousness, it becomes so much easier to let go of any feelings of ill will or any judgment you would typically make. Merely recognize that most people do not really know what they are saying or doing because their inner-self is in fact asleep and not observing or managing them. They are on auto-pilot as you once were.

As you increasingly develop the art of living, you will see that it is easier for YOU to manage your relationships with the people around you rather than letting them. Your intellect, emotions, or ego control you by focusing

and reacting to the worst aspects of the people around you. Identify the good that exists in everyone, or at the very least, understand that they are allowing their intellect, emotions, and ego to control them. It is a far more satisfying and productive starting point. It makes life so much easier on you, and you will achieve the best outcomes in doing so. Furthermore, you will notice your own development accelerates your increasing enlightenment, leading you to lasting happiness and stress-free life. In time, you may even find opportunities to help others find their inner self. Allowing them to develop the best in themselves and eliminate the worst, further contributing to a world that can move closer to peace and harmony.

The word karma is a useful reference here. The word is Sanskrit and means 'act', 'action,' 'deed.' The proposition is that people determine their own destiny through the quality of their acts: that is to say, we are all masters of our own fate. The more positive and pure that our actions are, the more positive and pure will be the fate of our own lives. Practice it for yourself and see if this is true. What have you got to lose?

Youth is wasted on the young (Wealth is wasted on the old!)

It appears as if life is not entirely structured in a way that works best for us. While we grow up in different environments and under different circumstances, for the most part, we all go through the same cycle as we grow.

1. Parents bring up their kids based on what they know of the world. Frequently, this is not that much! It's not their fault; it's just the way it is.
2. Kids go to school. This is good. A few are studious and engaged. Some are placed in the middle, as much interested in their social life or playing computer games. Some make little or no effort at all. Perhaps our first lesson at school should teach us why we should learn, and how to learn effectively while making the most of our free time. As it turns out, we are

left to work this out for ourselves.
3. Next, we are encouraged to go out and get a job. We spend years trying to earn as much money as we can to buy things, get married, and have kids. We get loans to buy houses and cars etc., etc.
4. Around forty or so, many experience a mid-life crisis wanting to unburden themselves of debt, get divorced (around 70% of us that is), drop the baggage and the possessions, and then wonder what we did with the first forty years of our life.
5. If we are lucky, we've managed to find the right person to be our partner by the time we get to our sixties and seventies. We have amassed some financial reserves (if it hasn't largely been lost in previous failed relationships), and we are in a position to take advantage of all the baggage we left behind. However, we are so exhausted by this time that all we want to do is stay home, watch TV, walk the dog and play bingo.
6. And then we die!

For the more senior readers of this book, a fair few of you will identify with this cycle. Either from your own first-hand experience or that of a friend. Now it is just a matter of making the most of what time is left and enjoying it as much as possible. Don't let the last years of your life slip away.

For the younger readers. Now is your chance to avoid sleepwalking onto the treadmill. Take time to speak with the older generation and listen carefully to what they say and the advice they give. It may not all make sense, but you are not limited to learning from your own mistakes. You can learn from the mistakes of others too, it's a lot less expensive! Do not sleepwalk through your life. Become present and aware and use your intellect to guide you. Life is for living and enjoying, not slaving yourself to your mind.

CHAPTER 4

Life is all about your actions - A note on jobs and careers

A fulfilling life is all about being active. How do we know this?

Exercise 7: Find a comfortable chair in your home. Sit down. Put this book down and do absolutely nothing. See how long it takes for you to want to get up and do something. You may wish to turn on the TV or continue rereading this book. You may want to go out and meet some friends. Whatever it is, at some point and generally quite quickly, there will be something.

No one can sit around and do absolutely nothing for regular and prolonged periods of time; we invariably get bored and fidgety. That's how we know that the natural state of all humans is to be active with some sort of endeavor. **One of the keys to lasting happiness is to embrace this knowledge and proactively, consciously direct your actions.**

Our lives are loosely segmented into four action categories: Work, Chores, Leisure, Sleep. How we label each action can be different for all of us. For example, some feel cooking is a chore, for others it is leisure, and so on. It applies to work as much as it does to leisure or chores. Indeed, as Confucius once said,

> "Choose a job that you love, and you will never have to work another day in your life."

It should be evident to most people, yet many do jobs they don't like because they feel they have no choice. For a few, this may be true, and the poverty trap does exist, but for the vast majority of us, the opportunity to change our lives and do work we genuinely enjoy exists. However, it takes time, effort, and the use of your intellect. For some reason, it seems that a good many people are just not prepared to allocate any of these resources. They are ready to slavishly carry out work that they don't enjoy merely paying the bills and surviving between their leisure times. In this scenario, people cause their own dissatisfaction, even if they blame it on something else. Many people's ego prevents them from blaming themselves for anything.

Working in a job you don't like solely for the income to buy more possessions or to satisfy your desires, or your ego's picture of success more often than not leads to stress and anxiety. It's a double whammy. You feel additional stress and anxiety from your job; the comforts and short-term pleasures you experience do not reduce your stress and anxiety or lead to lasting happiness. No wonder so many people reach a mid-life crisis. It is inevitable.

With so many different types of people in the world, with so many likes and dislikes, and with such a variety of skill sets, it is impossible to give career advice in a short paragraph that will suit all, other than to say, using your intellect and making an effort to find work that you genuinely enjoy is highly rewarding. Finding a job you love naturally supersedes the focus on any financial reward, high or low. The work you do becomes the reward in its own right. It may mean re-educating yourself or re-training, but ultimately it is worth the time and the effort. **Earning from a job that you love enables you to focus your attention effectively and deliver great work.** Doing great work allows you to advance in your career, and advancing your career invariably leads to greater returns.

Marco Pierre White, a British celebrity chef, expresses this well with his saying:

> "Perfection is a lot of little things done very well."

When you are passionate about what you do, you are far more inclined to focus on the details and ensure that everything that goes into what you do is done well.

CHAPTER 4

Thinking beyond jobs and careers - What is YOUR purpose in life?

As we go through school, we are brainwashed into thinking that we need to go out and get a job once we leave school. Some people do just that. They give zero consideration to what career they may be interested in pursuing, they merely want to leave school or university and get a job. Others do consider what career they want to pursue. They look at the longer term, go beyond the consideration of a particular job and map out a career path for themselves. Starting at the junior end of that path at the outset and then working their way up to what they consider to be the pinnacle of that particular career path. Others look at a career path more as a calling. Typically, careers such as teaching or charity work, nursing, or becoming an artist are considered more of a calling than a career. Yes, in almost all of these cases, most of us fail to consider purpose.

I expect most will have heard someone say the phrase "we all have a purpose in life" at some point or another and yet if you ask the person who said it what their purpose is they have no idea. Purpose should not be an unknown component of your life where you assume you have a reason to be but you do not know what it is. After all, if you do not know your purpose in life, how can you fulfill it? When you factor in purpose to your life and your actions, it changes everything. Not only does it allow you to tailor your actions, job, career, or calling to ensure positive contributions to society and the world around you, it also delivers a far greater sense of satisfaction and happiness for you too. Can you look at yourself now and say what your purpose in life is? Given that you have the power to determine your own purpose in life, what do you think it should be? What will your legacy be?

What makes more sense, spending less or more than you earn?

Of course, it is a loaded question, and in some ways, I am surprised this question needs to be asked. Yet, managing finances well is probably one of the best examples available for demonstrating that prevention is better than cure. In the words of Charles Dickens from his book David Copperfield, by the character Wilkins Micawber:

> "Annual income twenty pounds, annual expenditure nineteen pounds nineteen and six, result happiness. Annual income twenty pounds, annual expenditure twenty pounds nought and six, result misery."

It seems pretty obvious that spending more than you earn can lead to stress and anxiety, and it does. The number of people that go bankrupt each year is staggering. The potential stresses that result from going into debt cannot be overestimated. There are vast numbers of people that live the high-life financed by debt. All is well while they are managing to make their payments. Not so well if the payments dry up for some reason and the whole lot comes crashing down. Not to mention the run-of-the-mill, day-to-day stresses and strains that many experience just keeping up payments. Shakespeare also had a few words to say about debt in his play Hamlet:

> "Neither a borrower nor a lender be; for loan doth oft lose both itself and friend, and borrowing dulls the edge of husbandry."

Debt in itself is no bad thing, and we would not suggest that people should not borrow money but at the very least fully understand what you are getting yourself into and how deep you are going. If math is not your strong suit get someone to help you work the numbers. People often sleepwalk into spending more than they earn or take on more debt than they can safely manage in the belief that the comforts or pleasures that the debt buys can be managed and give rise to happiness or help them get to a better place in their life. Sometimes it does, sometimes it doesn't. Don't let overspending or going into debt be a source of stress and anxiety that you could easily avoid.

CHAPTER 4

What else do you need to know?

As noted at the outset, this chapter is designed to give you food for thought. In the complex world we live in today, there are so many things out there that can trigger stress, anxiety, and sadness. The ones in this chapter are just the tip of the iceberg. It is up to you to remain present, aware, and detached, at the same time remaining engaged, compassionate, and kind. Develop your intelligence and use your intellect to guide your actions in a way that gives rise to positive outcomes for you and all the people around you. Interpret your stream of experiences to guide your actions and reactions so that they become intelligent, deliberate, and measured.

Release the Power In You!

Chapter 5

Reader's Questions Answered

Before publishing this book, I gave copies of the first four chapters to various friends and family to get their reactions. The result was a flurry of good questions. Here are those questions together with their answers.

Q: What is the greatest obstacle to achieving success, lasting happiness, and a stress-free life?

A: Apathy.

   Some people put in the effort to learn and practice playing a musical instrument and enjoy the gift of playing music for the rest of their lives. Many do not. The same applies to learning how to get the most out of your life. Living is an art. The more you learn, the more you verify for yourself, the more you understand, and the more you practice, the easier it becomes. You need to put the effort in to get the results out. However, don't force it, experience it and enact it. Allow it to evolve little by little, or the journey will become a chore and source of anxiety in itself. It will come more easily to some than to others, like learning a second language. But if you relax and stick with it, achieving lasting happiness and living a stress-free life will result. If you decide not to make an effort and find yourself sad, stressed, and anxious, remember, you only have yourself to blame!

Q: Is it possible for a person to be physically or mentally restricted from enlightenment? If so, what might some of those restrictions be? If not, explain why it is universal.

A: For the vast majority of people there are no restrictions at all. All it requires is the right attitude toward personal development, an open mind, and the willingness to put in the effort needed to learn, verify and practice. The only exception is that anyone with learning difficulties, for whatever reason, may also experience difficulties learning to become enlightened. Even then, with assistance, it is possible for people with learning difficulties to pick up the basics and achieve a general improvement in their day-to-day living.

In reality, of course, there are plenty of people that do not have an open mind or they just have the wrong attitude to personal development, or they are just plain lazy.

> *"If you don't want to be educated, no one can help you. If you do want to be educated, no one can stop you."*

Q: *Even though I have found myself making good progress and I have already made significant improvements to my life, there are things that automatically make me feel stress and anxiety, particularly related to work and I find it hard to eliminate these feelings.*

A: This is entirely natural. Our egos and autonomic nervous systems are powerful forces. It is hard for most of us to fully eliminate feelings of stress or anxiety when certain external events happen, especially major events like losing your job, losing a home, or losing a loved one. During these times, you have to make even more effort to ensure you do not knee-jerk-react to what is going on around you. Practice remaining present and aware and stopping your mind from chattering. Use meditation and deep breathing exercises to help you relax and take control. Understand how to remain connected and yet detached, and work your way through the stress and anxiety. Taking an intellectual and practical approach rather than a purely emotional approach to stress and anxiety will help you work through these moments quicker and help you reduce the possibility of knee-jerk reacting and making things worse for yourself.

In simple terms, do everything you can just to let it go, re-group and move forward. It is remarkable how resilient and resourceful you can be when you give yourself the opportunity. You are also more likely to find that you provide the world and people around you with more opportunities to come to your aid and give you support when you do this. As with so many things that can cause us stress and anxiety, negative reactions do not give rise to positive outcomes.

CHAPTER 5

Q: I am human. I am going to be angry if someone steals my money, right?

A: Why? Anger is not a compulsory human response, it is a reaction and a choice. To start with, there is not one benefit to feeling anger ever. At best, anger makes you feel stress and anxiety, at worst, it can drive you to do something you will regret. Will anger help you get your money back? Then what purpose is getting angry going to serve?

If you practice renunciation, the ability to remain attached and yet detached from your money and possessions, then the loss will not affect you. If you feel anger toward the person, there is no need. Anyone who steals has clearly not reached any level of enlightenment and is sleepwalking through their lives trying to find ways to achieve happiness through things/possessions. Be sure in the knowledge that they will not achieve happiness this way. Perhaps you are angry at yourself for letting it happen. Let it go, detach yourself from your ego. As you say, you are indeed human, and as such, you must accept your fallibility. It is impossible to prevent all harm coming to you or others,

If you have not reached this level of enlightenment, and you feel anger brewing, the first thing to do is become present and aware and eliminate these feelings. Let the inner-you guide your intellect. Second, see if there is any reasonable action you can take to recover your loss. If yes, good. If not, accept the loss and move on.

Q: Are there any techniques that one can use to help stay present and aware?

A: It is quite usual at the outset to find yourself only able to stay present and aware for short periods of time, perhaps even a few seconds. Our chattering minds are so used to being in control that it takes time for the inner-you, your pure consciousness, to become the master. Furthermore, even when you are present and aware and have managed to pause your chattering mind, it is easy to get distracted or become absorbed in your day-to-day routine and forget to re-awaken the inner-you. I have used three techniques to help me:

1. I have found that a 10-15 minute period of slow breathing and awareness meditation just after I wake up is a good way to start each day. I make sure I bring myself fully present and aware following sleep, ensuring that my mind is at rest. I give myself time to fully awake and connect with my environment. Furthermore, I get up early and give myself plenty of time to prepare for the day ahead. No fuss, no rush, totally relaxed, and plenty of time to remain present and aware before facing what the day has to offer. If I notice myself getting overly distracted by work now and then during the day, I'll find time for another short meditation session to ensure the inner-me is in the driving seat, not my chattering mind.
2. Another technique I used was to train myself to become instantly present and aware if I found myself starting to knee-jerk-react to something going on around me that might ordinarily make me feel stressed or anxious. This enabled me to break the loop and take back control quickly, become present and aware and detach myself from whatever made me feel stressed. It was not easy at first, and sometimes I would even forget altogether and react. But with practice, it has become instant. It prevents me from knee-jerk-reacting to things when I am distracted or hyper-focused on some project or activity, eliminating any stress and anxiety.
3. Before writing this book, I made a series of notes highlighting the key points as a constant reminder. I found that having these notes close by at all times was a useful way to remind me regularly when I got distracted. Now I have copies of this book to remind me. One on my bedside table, one on my desk in the office, and even one on the coffee table in the lounge. If you make your own notes and keep them in places that you are likely to come across regularly, you too will find that these regular reminders will help you stay present and aware more often than not.
4. Something I still do is to take time out to just experience living. I have a full life. There is something I can be doing every minute of the day. I could happily keep going each day, bouncing from one activity to the next until it is time for bed. In the past, I would sit down for a while to

take a break. Shortly after, I would begin to feel a little bored and want to move on to the next activity or even look for a new activity to fill the gap. Now I enjoy times where I just sit, fully conscious, fully in the present, with my mind fully silent and savor all that is going on around me. It is similar to meditation with my eyes open while enjoying the experience of pure consciousness connected to everything around me.

Q: I can't quite figure out what is meant by being attached and detached simultaneously. I understand that this is important, but I can't work out how to experience it. Can you give me more to go on?

A: It took me years to fully understand this. For some reason, it just didn't resonate or connect with me, and then one day, it just clicked. Since then, fully understanding how to develop being both attached and detached has made a huge difference in my life and reduced feelings of stress and anxiety even further. I have been fortunate in my life to have owned many nice and expensive things. Once upon a time, it would have significantly disturbed me if I had lost or damaged any of these things. I would become quite frustrated, even angry at the loss, especially if someone else broke or lost any of them. I may even have directed my anger at them and been upset for some time. Now, no matter what, I have no such unhelpful attachments to things. If I lose or break anything I own, it does not bother me at all; it's just the way things are. Things get lost, and things get broken. You can expect it. If I have the money and I find the item useful, I may replace it. If not, then perhaps not. If I don't have the money, then no matter, I'll either learn to live without it or buy a cheaper version until perhaps one day I decide to replace it with the expensive version if I can. It doesn't matter either way; life is too short. I no longer worry or get stressed by such things.

With all that said, I still look after these things and still have sufficient attachment to these things to enjoy them. The same level of attachment and detachment can be applied to anything—your ego, people, your job, etc. Whenever you have a connection to something, you have a form of attachment to it. Putting that attachment into a constructive intellectual context is important. You do not have to turn yourself into a sociopath!

I am fortunate, I have not yet had to apply the same thinking to the people close to me. How would I cope if something were to happen to any of them? I hope that I will apply the same understanding, even to those closest to me. I know for certain that no amount of sadness, stress, anxiety, or outpouring of grief would bring any of them back or make me feel better. Why should I waste time and energy on such things? To show people how much I cared. That seems rather pointless and egotistical. I would rather celebrate my time with the person and bask in the joy and pleasures we once shared. I do hope I have reached that level of enlightenment when the time comes.

Q: What can I do if certain people get me down or stress me out?

A: By being present and aware, you allow the inner-you to observe and analyze the things in your life that cause you stress. That includes people. As I am sure everyone reading this is aware, people are way more complex to deal with than inanimate objects. Being able to manage and cope with stress is of great benefit. However, if you can avoid those things that you identify stress you out in the first place, then even better, prevention is better than cure.

If you find that certain people cause you sadness, stress, or anxiety, then quite simply, you only have two options. a) get yourself to a point where you can remain calm and stress-free under any circumstance, or b) avoid these people. If it is a boss or a colleague, consider a change. Perhaps a move to a different department or even a different company. You could even start up your own business. If it is a friend or family member, initially just spend less time with them and continue on your journey to enlightenment.

CHAPTER 5

Q: Seeing that this book is about awakening the inner-you, how do I truly analyze and work out what motivates the inner-me?

A: The inner-you is pure consciousness; pure existence. It is beyond the need to be motivated; it merely exists. Motivation is what drives your intellect to instruct your body to act. For example, if your brain senses that you are hungry and in need of sustenance, your intellect rationalizes this feeling and is motivated to move the body into action to find and eat food. When your mind controls you instead of the inner-you, your intellect is primarily motivated by a) your primal instincts (the need for food, shelter, and company, etc.), b) your desires; the need for pleasures and comfort, and c) your ego; your desire to shape the world or control people depending on the way your ego thinks the world should be. When you awaken the inner-you, your consciousness allows your intellect to decide what motivates it to act. If you are happy and no longer in desperate need of short-term pleasures or additional comforts, you will likely turn your attention to more altruistic pursuits. The key question to ask your intellect while being present and aware is 'what purpose do I want to have in life,' rather than what should I do with my life or how can I achieve wealth or fame? This is an opportunity for you to decide what your purpose in life should be.

One additional note to consider. Using words and thinking to describe and understand your consciousness is a bit like trying to use words to describe the sound of a bell. No words can ever replace or fully describe the 'experience' of hearing the sound of a bell. Trying to get your intellect to comprehend your consciousness in words will leave your mind chattering in circles forever. All you can do is relax, connect with, and 'experience' your existence, your inner-you. Allow that experience to flourish without effort. Increase your learning and apply your intellect; the rest will follow.

Q: What steps can I take to do a complete evaluation of myself?

A: This is not something you should worry about. This question is another example of how your mind is trying to rationalize things. Your mind is taking over, and you are trying to use your intellect and words to critique and evaluate yourself. The more instinctive and natural experiencing your life becomes, rather than thinking through your life, the process of a formal evaluation is no longer required. You will instinctively work out who you are and progressively shape yourself to the way you should be. Life is a journey, not a destination. Enjoy the journey. It is continuous and constantly changing until the day you pass away. Experience and enjoy every moment.

CHAPTER 5

Q: Is it possible to enjoy short-term pleasures without experiencing the negative feelings that come later? For Example, I'm out to buy a gaming device because it gives me pleasure. The future downsides of it crashing and failing or suddenly not working wouldn't bother me. I understand it's a machine and can fail. Yes, I'd be human and react, but my true feelings about it being nonoperational would be pretty nonchalant. I know it's not lasting happiness, but is it okay to seek those short-term pleasures if they affect your overall goal and thinking process?

A: There is absolutely nothing wrong with spending money buying things and enjoying short-term pleasures, although you will find that this becomes of less interest to you over time. Furthermore, if you are already detached sufficiently that the loss of your gaming machine would not phase you, then you are heading in the right direction.

The dangers can creep in at various stages of the process. For example, before you purchase the gaming machine, it can be an issue if you do not immediately have the money to purchase the device and spend your time yearning for the device, feeling anxious if you do not have it. This is a distraction, it leads to unhappiness, and it may even lead you to take action that may be detrimental to you or others. Perhaps you start thinking about taking someone else's machine or stealing the money from someone to purchase it. If you allow the desire to build up in your head, it can create significant stress and anxiety.

Further to this, you may decide you want to borrow the money to purchase the device. So many people around the world today owe considerable sums of money to the banks, which they have used to finance a life they cannot afford. This, too, can lead to stress and anxiety. You may find that you lose your job and cannot pay the money back. Or the machine does break, and you find yourself paying for something you no longer can use. Isn't it simpler to avoid the grief in the first place?

As you say, numerous potential stresses can evolve after you have purchased the machine, particularly if it does not live up to your expectations. But if you say that these negatives will not affect you, this is a good place to be. Yet, you did say, "Yes, I'd be human and react" well, this really boils down to what the level of your reaction is. If you decide to throw the machine through the window and send a parcel bomb to the manufacturer, this is what would consider an unnecessary gross over-reaction. If, on the other hand, you merely shrug your shoulders, speak out a mild cuss word and then see what you can do to rectify the situation calmly and intelligently without feeling stress or anxiety, then you are making excellent progress, and your life will be all the better for it.

Q: Who decides what 'living the right way is'?

A: You do!

It is important for you not to judge others or for others to make judgments of you. Much of it is common sense. Standards that society all agrees upon and why these guidelines appear in so many philosophical and religious texts. Some actions may require more training and more learning. Managing your income, for example, and learning about debt and finance. There are many scams and even legal traps out there that can lull you into taking action that seems good at the time but can lead you into taking action in a way that will be harmful to you in the future. This is where the value of education comes into its own. The smarter you become, the less likely you are to be caught out.

To guide you, there are several questions you can ask yourself before you do things, and if you are present, aware, and detached, you will know the true answer. These questions will guide you in deciding what the right action is to take to live the right way:

1. Will my action hurt or harm someone (or myself)? If the answer to this question is yes, there is a fair chance that it is the wrong thing to do.

2. What are the reasons for me doing this action? Analyze your true motives. If the answer is for selfish personal gain, to impede someone, to take advantage of someone, to put someone down, or revenge to get back at someone, again, this is probably not living the right way.
3. Could this action give rise to stress and anxiety for me or someone else in the future? Again, the answer will guide you.
4. Could this action give rise to a slew of unintended consequences?
5. Does the result of this action seem too good to be true? If the answer is yes, then it probably is.
6. What would I think if someone else took this action?

Being present and aware, turning your chattering mind off, removing your unhealthy attachments to things, especially your ego. Educating yourself, not taking what is presented to you at face value, and establishing a positive purpose for your life should give you all that you need to determine how to live your life the right way. Yep, it takes effort!

One final thing to remember. We are all human, and we all make mistakes; it is not possible to get it right all the time. When you make a mistake, do not obsess over it. Make what reasonable effort you can to correct the mistake if possible, then let it go, put it behind you, and move forward learning from your mistake.

Q: Is it wrong to WANT to grieve over the loss of a loved one? I recently lost a much-loved pet. This is not the first pet I have lost, and I was desperately upset and sad when my first pet passed. Now when I look at their photo, I remember my fondness and happy times, but I do not feel the same degree of sadness. I don't want to feel that way so quickly with my recent loss.

A: Actually, no. While over time it is possible to eliminate the need to grieve, grieving is a natural primal process. Indeed, crying is considered an important safety valve. Researchers have identified that crying releases oxytocin and endogenous opioids, also known as endorphins. These chemicals make you feel better and help ease physical and emotional pain. People often say,

> *"Have a good cry, you'll feel better."*

If your intellect is intelligently managing your grief and your grief is not driving you to act irrationally or recklessly in a way that will cause harm to you or another, then there is nothing wrong with this. Indeed, your grief is giving you context and even some degree of comfort as you celebrate the life of your pet.

There are many different types of loss. It could be your supercar blowing up on your driveway, losing money in a scam, loss of a pet, a close friend, or a family member. Your natural reaction to different losses will be different in each case and motivate your intellect to direct you to behave in different ways. The key to managing sadness, stress, and anxiety is not to let your grief, mind, and emotions control you. You do not have to put their memory in a box, lock it away and then move on as if they did not exist. It's more about carrying on with your life, keeping their memory with you, and remembering and celebrating the good times.

CHAPTER 5

Q: I understand that becoming aware and enlightened allows you to analyze each life experience logically and process it rather than 'knee-jerk-react to it. However, does showing less emotion make the enlightened person seem less human to others? I understand that an enlightened person won't care about this, but if you are to be a beacon for others to follow, how can this look enticing from the outside looking in?

A: As you say, the enlightened mind will not be concerned if people around them think they are not showing enough emotion in any given circumstance. That said, how people react to a person who is consistently calm and collected under any circumstance will also depend on the type of emotion you are referring to. If you mean anger, then most people will probably be rather impressed by the fact that you can remain cool under challenging circumstances. This is something to be admired. If you are referring to grief, remember that eliminating or managing grief does not mean that you have to be completely inhuman. You can still be compassionate and empathetic. Depending on the circumstance, perhaps providing comfort to and consoling those around you that are being emotional will also likely be seen as a positive. There are plenty of ways to conduct yourself that are entirely human without being visibly or overly emotional.

It is important to remember the separation between emotion and reaction. Or, to put it another way, between emotion and drama. Emotions are the feelings inside you. For the most part, people's reactions to their emotions are merely an autonomous act. Hence the expression,

> *"that person is such a drama queen"*

when we see someone who is overreacting. When you reach the point where you have modified your ego to eliminate negative emotions being formed in the first place, or to where you have sufficient control over your intellect through being present and aware you can guide your actions and reactions in ways that are more calm and collected, you will also have acquired the ability to guide your actions toward being kind, compassionate and giving. These reactions will be seen in a positive light. The more you practice the more apparent it becomes, the more you will instinctively understand, and the less you will worry about what others think.

Q: Does it matter if I create my own techniques to help me? I have found that once I have become present and aware, and analyzed a situation that may be causing me some angst I work out what advice I would give someone else in that situation and then move forward accordingly. I have managed to deal with a few circumstances and eliminate the angst this way.

A: No, not at all. The technique you describe is a good one. Rather than knee-jerk react or let the angst cause you ongoing stress, or get you to do or say something that you might regret, you have woken the inner-you to step and get the intellect to review the situation, come up with a practical and stress-free way to move forward in the form of advice to another, which in fact is advice for you. Asking 'what advice would I give to someone?' is a great question to ask. The net result; this situation is no longer causing you angst.

The purpose of this book is to act as an introduction and guide on how to live a successful, happy, and stress-free life. It is intended to give you enough information to continue the journey on your own. If you have gained enough knowledge to start experimenting with different techniques to help yourself, then this book has achieved its objective. As the saying goes,

"There is more than one way to skin a cat."

Acknowledgments

I would like to thank my wife, Kiron, for many things really, but primarily for making me want to be a better person.

I would also like to thank Trey for challenging my thinking all the way through the process of writing this book and helping me articulate the information in the book in a way that makes it simple for anyone to understand and follow.

Finally, I would like to thank Mike Starr for coming up with the expression, Youth is wasted on the young and wealth is wasted on the old.

About the Author

John was born in Bristol, the United Kingdom, in 1959. After studying Food Science and Technology for five years, he started work in Sales and Marketing in 1982, developing marketing strategies and turning them into actionable plans. John moved to Manama, Bahrain, in 1985, where he worked for a leading advertising agency for six years, working on some of the world's leading brands, including Unilever, KLM, and Qantas. He switched to another international agency in 1991 when he moved to Dubai, United Arab Emirates, working on General Motors and Pepsi Cola. He started his own advertising and marketing agency in 1995, working for a range of world-renowned clients, including Emirates, DP World, Standard Chartered Bank, and Géant Hypermarkets. In 2018 John moved to the United States, where he again started his own boutique advertising and marketing agency, working for a range of local and international clients and where he still works.

John's marketing career evolved from strategy development and client services to include scriptwriting, copywriting, video production, and photography. John spent many years understanding what motivates customers in order to create powerful advertising and marketing messages. During his time living in the Middle East, he traveled extensively across the US, Europe, and Asia and spent much time reading and studying theology and philosophy.

Made in the USA
Monee, IL
13 December 2021

8b66c1d1-af6d-4af8-b141-fb8c4e8079eaR01